Penguin Books
Your Pension

CW00921017

David Lewis is one of the country's most experienced personal financial writers. He is author of several books on investment, pensions, house purchase and insurance including *The Savers and Investors Guide* which is published annually by Wisebuy Publications and has sold over a quarter of a million copies. From 1976 to 1986 he was Editor of the *Daily Mail*'s *Money Mail* and previous to that was Editor of *Money Management* magazine. David Lewis is now an independent writer and editor and is currently involved in compiling a series of guides for independent financial advisers for *Financial Times Business Information*.

Norwich Union is a major British based group of companies operating principally in the world of insurance and pensions. The main company, the Norwich Union Life Insurance Society, is a mutual life office which distributes all its profits to the policy-holders and not to shareholders. The group offers a wide range of financial services – not only insurance cover for people and property but also endowment mortgage policies, pensions and other investment plans – with the stated aim of providing best value for money to present and future life policyholders. The assets of the Norwich Union group amount to well over £10,000 million.

Your Pension
The Norwich Union Guide

David Lewis

Penguin Books

PENGUIN BOOKS

Published by the Penguin Group
27 Wrights Lane, London W8 5TZ, England
Viking Penguin Inc., 40 West 23rd Street, New York, New York 10010, USA
Penguin Books Australia Ltd, Ringwood, Victoria, Australia
Penguin Books Canada Ltd, 2801 John Street, Markham, Ontario, Canada LR3 1B4
Penguin Books (NZ) Ltd, 182–190 Wairau Road, Auckland 10, New Zealand

Penguin Books Ltd, Registered Offices: Harmondsworth, Middlesex, England

First published 1988

Designed and produced by Wisebuy Publications, London

Typeset by MC Typeset Limited, Chatham, Kent
Made and printed in Great Britain by Richard Clay Ltd, Bungay

Contents

Acknowledgements   9

1 **How to retire rich**   11
A good deal. The new pension companies. Getting
advice on a pension. Where to get your pension.

2 **The different types of pension**   18
The State pension. Other pensions. A pension with
your job. A personal pension. Choose the type which
suits you.

3 **How pensions work**   23
Tax relief. Contribution limits. Tax free investments.
The combined effect of tax relief and tax exemption.
Converting your pension fund to a pension. The open
market option. The lump sum. Tax position on
retirement. Pension based on a wife's earnings. Why
a lump sum is worth taking. Choosing a retirement
date.

4   The State pension   41
State basic pension. State earnings related (additional) pension. An example. Home responsibilities protection. The reduced rate of national insurance. What
you pay for a State pension. Retirement age. What
you might get from the State. DHSS leaflets.

5   If you are an employee without a pension   59
Should you leave the State earnings related pension?
Comparing what you get from the State. Comparing
with a personal pension. In favour of opting out. In
favour of staying in. Minimum contribution personal
pension. More than the minimum. Saving towards a
tax free lump sum. How opting out works. An
example of opting out. How to leave the State
earnings related pension. A new job pension.

6   If you are already in a job pension   77
What you belong to. Final salary job pension. Money
purchase job pension. Contracted-out or in? Non-
contributory. Retirement age. Rising pension after
retirement. How long is it paid? Fringe benefits. Life
insurance. If you die before retirement. Ill or in an
accident. When you should leave. When you should
stay. Inland Revenue limits on a job pension.

**7   Additional voluntary contributions to a
job pension   94**
How to earn extra pension. Extra lump sum? Ordinary additional voluntary contributions. Free standing
additional voluntary contributions. Contracting-out.
Poor pension scheme.

8   How your money grows   101
Money purchase. Deposit based. Guaranteed or non-
profit. With-profits. Investment linking. Investment

funds: Cash deposit or money. Index-linked stock funds. Currency cash funds. Fixed interest fund (£ sterling). Property funds. Fixed interest funds (foreign). Mixed or managed funds. Equity funds. International funds. Broker funds. How to choose.

 9 **If you are self-employed**   **116**
Not much State pension. Retirement annuities. Extra or less lump sum. Retirement annuity or personal pension. When to pay contributions.

10 **If you own your own company**   **123**
Maximum contributions to a job pension. Inland Revenue limits on the maximum job pension. Personal pensions. Should you trade as a company? National insurance for husband and wife. Tax for husband and wife. When a personal pension is the right choice. When a job pension is better than a personal pension. Who should have the pension. Equalising pension in retirement. Which type of job pension.

11 **If you employ people**   **139**
Should you offer a pension? Non-contributory? Contract-out or in? Money purchase or final salary. Simplified job pension. Group personal pensions. Existing job pensions. Let employees do their own thing.

12 **Which pensions company?**   **149**
Independent financial advice. Comparative surveys. The basis for comparing. A process of elimination.

13 **Changing jobs**   **156**
Job pension transfers. Personal pension transfers. Retirement annuity transfers. Refund of contributions.

8

14 Life insurance with tax relief   **165**
Do it yourself. Tax relief on life insurance. Avoiding
probate and inheritance tax.

15 Pension mortgages and loan backs   **172**
Pension mortgages. Pension company loan back.
Bank loan back. The snags.

Glossary   **181**

Appendix 1:   How money grows: lump sums.   **200**

Appendix 2:   How money grows: yearly
investments   **202**

Appendix 3:   How inflation reduces the value of
your investments.   **204**

Appendix 4:   The Financial Services Act.   **206**

Index   **209**

Acknowledgements

My thanks go to everyone who helped me write this book. These include the Company Pensions Information Centre and the DHSS Information Division whose department kindly checked details concerning the State pension. To Ken Hurst, John Brister and John Blanchard at Norwich Union for organising some of the tables and for helping check the facts. To Mark Daniel of Equitable Life for supplying information for some of the tables and teaching me how compound interest works. And to David Norris of chartered accountants Bennett Nash Woolf for checking my arithmetic on national insurance and tax for a company.

On the production side my thanks to Susan Lewis for editing the text and making it more understandable. To Karen Banks for helping compile the tables in the Appendix. And to Andrew Franklin, Executive Editor of Penguin books who masterminded this whole project.

David Lewis, May 1988

1
How to retire rich

Everyone wants a comfortable retirement without financial worries. A steady income to maintain your standard of living with enough money to run the car, take a good holiday or two each year and pay for the luxuries you feel entitled to. A time to reflect and potter about without the nagging worry of an inadequate income to keep you in the way you want.

Fewer and fewer people live on the basic State retirement pension alone. Those who do, wish they didn't. Getting by on £41 a week or £66 a week for a married couple is not something to look forward to on the day you finish work after toiling hard for 40 years or more. At the other end of the spectrum, if you work in the public sector or for a large paternalistic employer you may imagine you are already well provided for in your retirement. You may be but only if you remain in your employer's pension scheme for 40 years and you are certain you will stay with them until you retire.

Getting a good pension at retirement is largely a question of what you can afford to save while you are still working. Most people never really consider pensions as important until they reach the age of 40. Even then many prefer a good holiday to putting the money aside for a pension. Although they probably feel different as they near 50. Indeed under the new pensions legislation it is possible to start drawing a pension at 50. But saving in the right way can make a great deal of difference to the pension which you will get on retirement.

So be sensible about your aspiration to retire rich. Use this book to find out all about saving towards a pension for your, hopefully, wealthy retirement. Get all the information you require, work out how much you can afford to save now, and the best type of scheme for your circumstances. The earlier you start contributing towards a pension, the richer you will be when you retire.

A good deal

When I was Editor of the *Daily Mail's* Money Mail pages from 1976 to 1986 we constantly campaigned for a better deal for pensions, especially for people who changed or lost their job. Under headlines like "Free us from the pensions trap" and "Give us the chance to get out", we drew attention to the priviliged position of public sector employees like local authority and civil service employees who were given inflation-linked pensions and full transferibility while people in the private sector lost out severely if they changed or lost their job.

We urged the Government to improve matters but despite a report published in 1981 by The Occupational Pensions Board, a Government advisory body, which suggested improvements, little was done due to the implacable opposition of some sections of the pensions industry. They should have been less resistant to change because the changes finally coming into effect on the day this book is published are far more radical than anyone would have dreamed of when we started our campaign over ten years ago.

Back in 1983 in an article on pension planning I wrote:

"Let's hope that when a change comes it gives us more freedom of choice rather than a mass of complicated rules . . ." The new rules do offer more freedom of choice. But they also contain a lot of complicated rules which I explain in this book.

The new pension companies

Pensions used to be provided mainly by life insurance companies. From 1 July 1988 this changes as new pensions rules come into effect and new laws governing investment advice are introduced under the Financial Services Act. Now banks, building societies and unit trusts can also offer pensions to the public though a life company needs to be involved when the pension starts to be paid. While this will raise the number of pensions companies, sometimes called *pensions providers*, and possibly increase competition, it does not necessarily offer individuals any better way to invest their money.

The tax exemptions apply to all organisations in exactly the same way. So unlike other types of investments, you do not need to concern yourself with whether your pensions company is a life insurance company or a bank or a building society or a unit trust. Instead you can concentrate on the type of pension you are considering.

Getting advice on a pension

The Financial Services Act has brought into effect important rules which affect anyone seeking or giving advice on saving towards a pension. These rules apply to most pensions and investments but from now on they are discussed only with reference to pensions.

All advisers must decide whether they are either *independent advisers* offering a choice of the best pensions products from all the companies on the market or whether they wish to act as an *appointed* or *tied* agent to a single company. This concept is known as *polarisation*. How pensions companies are regulated under the Financial Services Act is described in *Appendix 4*.

In practice banks, building societies and other branch organisations can be both *independent advisers* and *appointed agents* by acting solely as an appointed agent in their branches but owning another company which contacts its clients by post or is referred by the branch which is an independent adviser. This is allowed although many in the business believe it should not be. Banks and building societies as well as offering their own deposit based pension schemes can act as agents for life insurance companies and unit trust groups. Many including some quite large ones have decided to become appointed agents of just one pensions company. Others have chosen to become independent advisers.

Appointed agents can only recommend the products of the single company they represent. Independent advisers are supposed to recommend the best pension on the market for you. **It is obvious that unless you have the means of finding the best product on the market for yourself without the help of anyone else, you should get advice from an independent adviser rather than an appointed agent.** If you are in doubt as to the status of your adviser, ask him or her which category they are in.

Best advice

All investment advisers are now supposed to give *best advice*. If they are *independent advisers* they are supposed to research the market, read published surveys of investment products or do their own. They are not supposed to be influenced by the commission they receive.

If the adviser is an *appointed agent* he or she can only give you advice about the products of the company he or she exclusively represents. In that case the advice must still be 'best' in so far as you must be recommended the product which is suitable for your needs and objectives, and, theoretically, if the appointed agent's company does not offer it, he or she should say so. The snag is that they are not then allowed to recommend another company.

Independent advisers

The following banks and building societies have announced that they are to be *independent advisers*:

Alliance & Leicester	Marsden
Bank of Scotland	Melton Mowbray
Birmingham Midshires	National & Provincial
Bradford & Bingley	National Westminster
Bristol & West	Nationwide Anglia
Britannia	Northern Rock
Cheltenham & Gloucester	North of England
Halifax	Royal Bank of Scotland
Ipswich	Saffron Waldon & Essex
Lambeth	West Bromwich
Leamington Spa	Woolwich
Leeds Permanent	Yorkshire Building Society
Leek United & Midlands	

Tied agents

The following have subsidiary companies which are *independent advisers* but advice in a branch is as an *appointed agent*. If you want independent advice you must ask your bank or building society branch to refer you to the subsidiary company which is an independent adviser.

Abbey National	National County (no
Barclays	advice given at branches)
Clydesdale	Skipton
Co-operative	TSB
Lloyds	Yorkshire Bank (no
Midland	advice given at branches)

This may give you the rosy impression that you will receive the 'right' investment advice from anyone who offers you advice. Unfortunately there is little agreement on what constitutes the 'right' advice let alone 'best' advice. The new rules have only just come into effect and it is likely to be some time before they have a significant effect on the quality of advice given. In any event you cannot legislate for good judgement. An adviser can only give advice. It is up to you to accept or reject that advice and it is you, the investor, who must make the final decision about what is best for you.

Financial information

Advisers must ask for a minimum amount of financial and personal information from you, the client, or have it on file, before they give advice. This is known as *know your client*. If you don't want to give the adviser this information – you may feel you know exactly what you want – then you have to sign a form saying you don't want to tell the adviser. Signing the form though, rids advisers of responsibility of giving you wrong advice because they didn't know your detailed circumstances.

Record keeping

Advisers of all types now have to keep records on the advice they give and details of their clients' circumstances. They must note down what advice they give, even if it is verbal, and the reasons for giving it. They must also keep records of the information they have used, for instance published surveys, to give advice, and they must ensure that they don't use out of date information. The records have to be supplied to regulatory bodies in the event of a complaint.

Where to get your pension

There is no 'best buy' pension scheme – at different ages or for different amounts or for different types of pension scheme, quite a number of different pensions companies will fall into the recommended category. For that reason it is essential to find an adviser who is not linked exclusively to one company but who can shop around.

All members of *FIMBRA*, Financial Intermediaries and Brokers Regulatory Association, are in that position and so are *Insurance Brokers*. With other advisers you have to find out – for instance banks and building societies consult the list on the previous page but check that the bank or building society is still an independent adviser when you seek advice. Some have been having second thoughts and it is likely that quite a few building societies will convert from being independent advisers to appointed agents over the next few years; they are unlikely to make a big song and dance about it.

Chartered Accountants and *Solicitors* will usually be independent advisers. Ask what the adviser's status is before you get involved.

2
The different types
of pension

You can save towards a pension using any means of savings or investment. But if you are certain the money you are saving is for your retirement, and you are also certain that you will not need it earlier, then it is much more sensible to save towards a pension through a pension scheme as there are tremendous tax saving advantages by doing this. These advantages are explained in **Chapter 3 How pensions work**.

You can get a pension from the State, through your job, from your own extra contributions to your job pension or you can make your own arrangements through a personal pension.

This Chapter gives a brief summary description of the different types of pension to enable you to distinguish one from the other. It also gets you used to the more important names which you need to get to grips with if you are to get the best deal from your pension. More details are given in later Chapters depending on your circumstances.

The State pension

You get this by paying national insurance contributions.

Normally unless you are earning very little these contributions are compulsory. The State pension comes in two main parts. The first is the *State basic pension* which everyone who pays enough contributions is entitled to. If you are not working you are allowed to make voluntary contributions to the State basic pension.

The second is the *State earnings related (additional) pension*, also known as *SERPS*, which is only available to employees. You are allowed to opt out of the State earnings related (additional) pension if you belong to certain types of pension scheme with your job or if you choose to have part of your national insurance contributions paid instead to your own *personal pension*.

Chapter 4 The State pension tells you what you can expect from your State pension, both basic and earnings related. **Chapter 5 If you are an employee without a pension** gives you the points for and against opting out of the State earnings related (additional) pension. In **Chapter 6 If you are already in a job pension** you can find out what happens if you are in a job pension which has opted out of the State earnings related (additional) pension.

Other pensions

Although other types of pension differ in detail, they are overall treated in the same way with big tax advantages. **Chapter 3 How pensions work** describes these advantages and gives the contributions limits and pension limits for the different types of job and personal pensions.

A pension with your job

Many firms, especially large companies, run pension schemes for their employees. In the past these were often compulsory but since April 1988 you have the right not to belong to a scheme run by your employer. They are often called *company* or *occupational pensions*.

Pensions with your job can be *non-contributory* or *contributory*. Non-contributory means that your employer pays the whole cost of the pension – a good deal provided the pension has reasonable benefits. Contributory means that you pay towards the pension yourself, often 5% of your pay; your employer also pays towards your pension.

Job pension schemes are either *final salary* or *money purchase:*

● Final salary means the pension you get is worked out according to the number of years you have been in the pension scheme and your pay shortly before you retire. The maximum is usually around two thirds of your final pay if you have been in the same scheme for 40 years.

● Money purchase means that your pension depends on the amount of money which is put aside for you in your own *pension fund* or *pension account*: the money you and your employer contribute is accumulated with interest and capital gains. At retirement this is used to buy a guaranteed income for life called an *annuity* or a *pension annuity* from a life insurance company.

If you are already in a job pension scheme but you don't think you will be getting a large enough pension, you can top it up with *additional voluntary contributions* sometimes abbreviated to *AVC*. These additional voluntary contributions are usually on a money purchase basis even if the main scheme is worked out on your final pay. They are paid into a special scheme chosen by your employer but subject to the rules of the main scheme.

There has recently been a new type called *free standing additional voluntary contributions* (or free standing AVC) where the contributions are made to a pensions company of your choice, not to the scheme your employer has chosen. Free standing additional voluntary contributions are always on a money purchase basis. More on this in

Chapter 7 Additional voluntary contributions to a job pension.

Chapter 6 If you are already in a job pension covers all the different types of job pension schemes from the point of view of employees. **Chapter 10 If you own your own company** describes how company directors can set up their own job pension just for themselves. **Chapter 11 If you employ people** looks at job pensions from a small employer's point of view and the various options you can take. It explains the different types of money purchase job pensions including *contracted-in money purchase, contracted-out money purchase* also known as *COMPS, simplified money purchase, group personal pensions* and *final salary* pension schemes.

A personal pension

Since 1 July 1988 a new type of pension is available to nearly everyone. A personal pension is a means of saving towards retirement which is individual to you. It is always on a *money purchase basis* – ie your pension is based on what you save and how much it grows in value.

A personal pension is not tied to a job – and changing jobs makes no difference to the eventual pension you get. Pensions, called *retirement annuities* (or self-employed pensions) which are rather like personal pensions, have been available to the self-employed and people who did not belong to a company pension in the past. But in the past problems were encountered when you moved jobs or moved in and out of self-employment. **Chapter 3 How pensions work** gives a lot of information on how personal pensions work and **Chapter 9 If you are self-employed** discusses how the self-employed should plan their pensions and the differences between the old *retirement annuity* and the new personal pensions.

As a means of promoting personal pensions and encouraging people to make their own private pensions provision and to rely less on the State at retirement, the Government has decided to allow people to make their own choice as to whether they want to stay in the State earnings related (additional) pension. Unfortunately the rules are very complex and are rather difficult to understand. They are described in **Chapter 5 If you are an employee without a pension**. You don't have to opt out of the State earnings related (additional) pension in order to take a personal pension.

Choose the type or combination which suits you

There is no best type of pension; there is only the best type of pension for you. By the time you have finished this book, sought advice and made your own enquiries, you will have a good idea of what is best for you.

Don't ignore the possibility that you may be eligible for more than one type of pension. For instance if you have two jobs, you can belong to one type for one job and another for the second. And if you belong to a job pension scheme you are allowed to make additional voluntary contributions yourself as well. If you are self-employed in your spare time you can also be eligible to take out a personal pension. There are a great many different ways in which a *money purchase* pension can accumulate your money. The choice of the right way for you is very important and is covered in **Chapter 8 How your money grows**.

3
How pensions work

A pension is a regular payment received by someone when they retire, normally in return for contributions. With the State pension your eligibility depends on the national insurance contributions you pay on your earnings. With a pension from your job, contributions are deducted from your pay. And if you are your own boss or choose to make your own arrangements, then you make contributions to a personal pension by cheque or standing order or direct debit through your bank account.

Tax relief

The State pension apart, all types of pension scheme are treated in broadly the same generous way for tax. The contributions you make to the scheme are eligible for full tax relief. That means for every £100 you pay, you get a tax rebate. If you are a basic rate taxpayer that is worth 25% of what you have invested. For every £100 you invest, your rebate is worth £25, so the actual cost is £75.

If you are a higher rate taxpayer you get tax relief at the 40% higher rate of tax. So if your tax rate is 40% then for each £100 you pay in contributions, you get a rebate of £40 so the cost of your contribution is only £60.

Contribution limits

With all pension schemes there are limits on how much you can pay in – or on the benefits you can draw when you retire.

The State pension scheme

This is compulsory unless you are on very low earnings. You can opt out of the earnings related part of it though – and this is discussed in later chapters.

Personal pensions

Personal pensions, and their predecessors *retirement annuities* which are now only available to people who already have existing policies, have a scale of contributions related entirely to your earnings. You are allowed to pay up to 17.5% of your *net relevant earnings* (that's usually earnings which don't count towards a job pension scheme) in each tax year. There are higher limits once you reach the age of 50. And you can continue to pay contributions until you reach your 75th birthday. The limits are given in the table on page 26. Up to 5% of your earnings can be in contribution towards a life insurance policy which has a term which ends before you reach the age of 75. The 5% limit is included in the 17.5% limit, it is not additional. More information on life insurance in **Chapter 14 Life insurance with tax relief**.

Carry forward of allowances You don't have to pay the contributions in the tax year in which you gain the 17.5% or whatever tax allowance. You can carry forward the allowances for up to six tax years.

For example suppose you earned £10,000 a year in each of the past six tax years and you were neither in a job pension nor a personal pension during that period. Each year you have an allowance of 17.5% of your earnings. So 17.5% of £10,000 is £1,750. As your earnings were unchanged, then you have allowances of seven times £1,750 which totals £12,250 which you can put into a personal pension. It is seven rather than six because you also have an allowance for the current tax year.

Twelve thousand pounds is more than your income so you obviously cannot afford to pay such a large contribution – or can you?

If you have just inherited money from an elderly relative, putting the money into a personal pension would be an ideal investment. Suppose you decide to invest £10,000. This is reduced by the pensions company's initial charge – typically 5% or £500 in this case. So you have an investment in a pension worth £10,000 minus £500 equals £9,500. But you get tax relief on your personal pension – for a contribution of £10,000 you can deduct the basic rate of tax, say 25%, which means you actually pay £7,500. So you have an investment of £9,500 at a cost to you of £7,500 – an immediate profit of £2,000!

You don't have to inherit or have money to make use of your unused contributions. If you have a home where the mortgage is relatively low in relation to its current value, the pensions company will often lend you the money; there is more on this in **Chapter 15 Pension mortgages and loan backs**.

When you make a pension contribution which is more than the allowance for the tax year in which it is made, you count firstly as having used up the allowance in that tax year. Then you can use unused allowances from previous tax years up to six years earlier, starting with the earliest first.

Tax relief as if last year You can opt to have the contributions you pay in the current tax year treated as being paid in the previous tax year. That is mainly an advantage if you are a higher rate taxpayer: you can wait until after the end of a tax year when you know exactly what your income will be before deciding the amount of contributions you wish to make in that year.

If you do this the contribution you opt to treat as being paid in the previous year cannot use up allowances you have received in the actual year it is paid in – only allowances from previous years. However using allowances from previous years means that in practice you can go back seven years rather than six.

Table 1

Personal pensions contribution limits as % of salary

For the 1988–89 and 1987–88 tax years Age at start of tax year	%
50 and under	17.5
51 to 55	20.0
56 to 60	22.5
61 to 75	27.5

For earlier tax years[1] Year of birth	%
1934 or later	17.5
1916–1933	20.0
1914–1915	21.0

[1] Since 1982–83

Pensions from your job

These have different contribution limits. Employees are only allowed to make contributions of up to 15% of their earnings in the tax year. But employers can generally contribute as much as they like – though there are limits on the pension which can be paid on retirement; the limits are related to how long you have been working for the organisation. More details are given in **Chapter 6 If you are already in a job pension**. The 15% limit consists of contributions to the main pension scheme and includes any *additional voluntary contributions* you make.

Tax free investments

Money accumulating in all pension schemes is one of the few investments which are truly tax free. They are free from all personal and company taxes. Neither you, nor the pension company, pay any income tax, capital gains tax or corporation tax on the income and profits which accumulate in your pension scheme. Other investments are often claimed to be *tax exempt* when in reality they are just *tax paid*. Tax paid means the investment company has to pay tax but you do not have to pay any extra. With pensions the pensions company pays no tax.

This tax exemption is very valuable indeed and, together with tax relief on the contributions, is the major reason for saving towards retirement through a pension rather than using other types of investment.

This is easily illustrated by an example. Suppose you have £9,500 invested in your pension fund (that is £10,000 less £500 deducted as an initial charge by the pensions company) and this grows at an average of 10% a year. After 20 years your money grows to £63,911, a profit of £53,911. But if you had to pay 25% tax on the profit that means that 25% of £53,911 goes in tax (that's £13,478) leaving you with £40,433 profit which is quite a lot less. If you are a higher rate taxpayer you make an even greater saving.

The combined effect of tax relief and tax exemption

Now let's look at the combined effect of tax relief and tax exemption. Suppose you have £10,000 to invest. As demonstrated in the example of tax relief above, suppose that £10,000 gets relief at 25% so the cost of your pension is only £7,500. The pensions company invests your £9,500 (having taken the £500 charge) and gets a return of 10% a year for 20 years accumulating a sum of £63,911.

What happens if you do it yourself outside the pension company. You invest the same amount as your pension scheme cost you after tax relief which is £7,500. Suppose that is invested in exactly the same way but the profits are taxed at 25%. So the £7,500 (less the 5% initial charge of the investment company which would be £375) gives an investment of £7,125. This grows at only 7.5% a year for 20 years which accumulates a sum of £30,266.

So tax relief and tax exemption for someone who pays tax at 25% more than doubles the amount of money available to earn you a pension. With a pension scheme you end up with £63,911 which can be used to get a pension annuity. Whereas in a similar investment not in a pension scheme you accumulate £30,266. **This should make you very seriously consider saving towards retirement through a pension rather than by any other means**.

If you pay higher rate tax, the difference is even more spectacular. For instance if you get tax relief at 40% on a £10,000 investment, at a cost of £6,000, £10,000 (less the pension company's initial 5% charge of £500 which is £9,500) can be invested in a pension scheme. At 10% a year this grows to £63,911 over 20 years.

Suppose you, a higher rate taxpayer invest the same amount (£6,000) in an ordinary investment. After the 5% charge this gives £5,700. But most ordinary investments are then taxed at 40% rather than 25%. So instead of accumulating at 7.5% a year as for a basic taxpayer, for a higher rate taxpayer the fund accumulates at a mere 6% a year after tax. After 20 years this gives a fund of £18,280 which compares with £63,911 for a higher rate taxpayer saving towards retirement through a pension scheme. That is three and a half times as good as saving towards retirement by any other means.

Table 2
How tax relief and tax exemption help your pension fund grow

Lump sum invested after tax relief: £	Fund accumulates at 10% a year for 20 years			
	Other similar savings and your tax rate is:		In a pension scheme and your tax rate is:	
	25% £	40% £	25% £	40% £
500	2,018	1,523	4,261	5,326
1,000	4,036	3,047	8,522	10,651
5,000	20,177	15,233	42,607	53,259
10,000	40,355	30,468	85,215	106,519

Yearly contribution for 20 years after tax relief: £	Fund accumulates at 10% a year for 20 years			
	Other similar savings and your tax rate is:		In a pension scheme and your tax rate is:	
	25% £	40% £	25% £	40% £
100	4,422	3,704	7,980	9,975
500	22,112	18,522	39,902	49,877
1,000	44,225	37,043	79,803	99,754
2,000	88,450	74,086	159,606	199,508

Note: Assumes 5% charge deducted at outset. These figures do not take account of inflation which at 3.5% a year would cut their value in today's money by just under half.

Converting your pension fund to a pension

Unless you are in a pension through your job which is based on your salary, your pension is *money purchase* and based on the accumulated value of your contributions (and your employers' if he makes them) plus interest and capital gains which are accumulated.

When you want to start to draw the pension (and often you have a choice of retirement date see below) you have to convert your accumulated pension fund into a pension by buying a *pension annuity*. An annuity is a guarantee by a life insurance company to pay you a pension for the rest of your life.

The amount of pension you get from the annuity obviously depends on how large a lump sum you have accumulated in your pension fund. It also depends on:

● Your age when you start to draw it (it is higher the older you are)

● Whether you are a man or a woman (it is higher for a man of the same age as a woman)

● Whether you want it guaranteed to be paid for a fixed number of years, say five or ten, even if you die within that period in which case the pension is paid to whoever you tell the trustees to give it to or you leave it to in your will (it is lower if you choose this option)

● Whether you want a pension to be paid to your widow and how much (it is lower if you do)

● Whether you want an increasing pension, say 4% or 5% a year or one linked to the index of retail prices or one which is with-profits and is linked to profits of the insurance company (in all these cases it is much lower if you do). Examples are given in the table.

● How frequently the pension is paid (paid yearly is higher than paid half yearly which is higher than paid quarterly which is higher than paid monthly)

How it works Suppose you have accumulated £100,000 in your pension fund. You use this to buy your pension annuity. Based on Table 3 overleaf at age 65 a fund of £100,000 could buy a man a fixed pension annuity of £13,361 a year. But if he wants a pension which rises by 4% a year, he only gets a pension of £10,554 at the outset.

Pension annuity rates depend on interest rates at the time when you buy the annuity so they may vary from the examples given here. If interest rates fall, then annuity rates fall, if they rise, then annuity rates rise. However once the annuity has been bought, the rate is guaranteed and your pension will not fall except in the case of a with-profits pension which can fall if profits do not come up to expectation.

The open market option

Only life insurance companies issue pension annuities. That means that if your pension has been accumulating with a pensions company which is not a life company, when you want to retire you have to find a life company to use the proceeds of your pension fund to buy the pension annuity.

Even if your pensions company is a life insurance company, you don't have to take the pension annuity it offers – you can usually shop around and try and do better elsewhere. This is called the *open market option.*

The lump sum

You can normally take a *cash lump sum* instead of part of your pension. There is no tax to pay on this lump sum. Although it is called a 'cash' lump sum, you will be paid by cheque.

Table 3
How much pension annuity your accumulated fund will buy

Age when you start pension	Fixed[3] £	Increasing at 4% a year[1,3] £	Index-linked £	With-profits[2] £
Man				
50	10,769	7,494	5,823	10,890
55	11,430	8,431	6,563	11,547
60	12,264	9,357	7,487	12,373
65	13,361	10,554	8,678	13,449
70	14,782	12,098	10,197	14,826
75	16,541	14,012	12,058	16,496
Woman				
50	10,160	6,803	5,132	10,280
55	10,576	7,511	5,662	10,696
60	11,174	8,206	6,372	11,294
65	12,026	9,155	7,330	12,141
70	13,221	10,459	8,628	13,319
75	14,848	12,219	10,359	14,899
Joint man and woman of same age				
50	9,757	6,381	4,734	9,877
55	10,030	6,963	5,156	10,152
60	10,442	7,491	5,720	10,569
65	11,064	8,228	6,488	11,196
70	11,991	9,270	7,550	12,127
75	13,342	10,740	9,022	13,472

Assumes accumulated pension fund is £100,000 and pension is paid monthly in arrears and guaranteed for five years. [1]Figures for pension in first year. [2]Assumes 6.5% bonus rate; if bonus is less the pension could fall; if more it will rise; current bonus rate 7.5%: [3]Assumes 10% non-enhanced immediate annuity rates. Source: Norwich Union (fixed and 4% a year), Equitable Life: (index-linked and with-profits).

Personal pensions

For personal pensions this cash lump sum is a maximum of 25% of the accumulated pension fund with a maximum of £150,000 from any one pension plan. So if you have accumulated £100,000 in your pension fund, you can take £25,000 as a cash lump sum and the other £75,000 must be used to buy a pension annuity.

There is no lump sum available on the part of your personal pension accumulated from national insurance contributions which you have opted to have paid into a personal pension instead of the State earnings related (additional) pension. But it can raise the lump sum from other contributions. More details on this on page 68 in **Chapter 6 If you are an employee without a pension**.

Job pensions

For job pensions the cash lump sum is worked out as a proportion of your *final salary*. Final salary is based on your salary before tax and national insurance. But final salary does not mean your last wages or salary payment before you retire. It is normally the higher of:

● The average of your salary over any three or more consecutive years ending not more than ten years before retirement

● Your salary in any single year in the five years prior to retirement.

The point of these rules is to prevent people whose earnings have fallen in the ten years before retirement from having to receive a lower pension or lump sum. If you own or control more than 20% of the shares in the company you work for (or have in the past ten years) or earn over £100,000 a year, the first definition is used.

The maximum cash lump sum also depends on whether you can take the maximum pension you are allowed to under the Inland Revenue limits. You may not have paid enough into the pension scheme or the scheme rules do not entitle you to take the maximum lump sum or pension allowed. If you cannot take the maximum pension you are entitled to, you have to take a lower proportion of your accumulated pension fund as a cash sum. Table 4 opposite shows the range of cash lump sum you can draw when you retire. Many schemes only allow the minimum lump sum. The Inland Revenue limits on the maximum pension you can get are explained in detail in **Chapter 10 If you own your own company** and also in **Chapter 6 If you are already in a job pension**.

This complex formula based on your final salary applies even if the pension scheme to which you belong is *money purchase* where the amount of pension and lump sum you receive has nothing to do with your salary.

The maximum cash lump sum you can take if you joined a pension scheme on or after 17 March 1987 is £150,000; there is no overall limit if you joined before that date. There is no cash lump sum for *additional voluntary contributions* which you started to make on or after 17 March 1987 nor for *free standing additional contributions*. These schemes are explained in **Chapter 7 Additional voluntary contributions to a job pension**.

Tax position on retirement

With all this talk of tax relief and tax exemption you might expect your pension to be tax free too. Unfortunately that is not the case. A pension once it starts to be paid is liable to income tax at whatever rate you pay on your other income. The good news is that all pensions are exempt from national insurance contributions.

Like everyone else, if you draw a pension you don't have to pay tax on the first so much of your income. These are called *personal allowances* and there are different ones for

Table 4

How much cash lump sum with a pension from your job

Years of service	Range of lump sum as a proportion of your final salary	
	Minimum[1]	Maximum[2]
1 to 8	3/80ths for each year	
9	27/80ths to	30/80ths
10	30/80ths to	36/80ths
11	33/80ths to	42/80ths
12	36/80ths to	48/80ths
13	39/80ths to	54/80ths
14	42/80ths to	63/80ths
15	45/80ths to	72/80ths
16	48/80ths to	81/80ths
17	51/80ths to	90/80ths
18	54/80ths to	99/80ths
19	57/80ths to	108/80ths
20	60/80ths to	120/80ths
21	63/80ths to	120/80ths
22	66/80ths to	120/80ths
23	69/80ths to	120/80ths
24	72/80ths to	120/80ths
25	75/80ths to	120/80ths
26	78/80ths to	120/80ths
27	81/80ths to	120/80ths
28	84/80ths to	120/80ths
29	87/80ths to	120/80ths
30	90/80ths to	120/80ths
31	93/80ths to	120/80ths
32	96/80ths to	120/80ths
33	99/80ths to	120/80ths
34	102/80ths to	120/80ths
35	105/80ths to	120/80ths
36	108/80ths to	120/80ths
37	111/80ths to	120/80ths
38	114/80ths to	120/80ths
39	117/80ths to	120/80ths
40	120/80ths	

[1]When actual pension is below Inland Revenue maximum limits. [2]When actual pension is equal to Inland Revenue maximum pension. Lump sums for people who joined a pension scheme before 17 March 1987 are according to a less restrictive scale.

married, single, and higher ones for people on modest incomes from the tax year in which you or your wife reach your 65th and 80th birthdays.

State pensions have no tax deducted from them but they are taxable (unless you are disabled and continue to draw invalidity benefit after pension age). So if you start your pension after State pension age, then a large part of your allowances will be set against the State pension. If you retire early, then the allowances can be set against your personal or job pension.

Job pensions are paid through PAYE like your pay. You will be given a code number to determine how much tax is paid which means the tax deducted will vary according to any other income or pensions you have and whether tax is deducted from that income before you get it. If your pension is very large, higher rate tax as well as basic rate tax will be deducted.

Personal pensions and retirement annuities have basic rate tax deducted from the payments which are sent to you. If you are not liable to tax on them or on all of them, you can claim a rebate from the Inland Revenue. If you are liable to higher rate tax you will get a tax assessment once a year in the Autumn relating to the previous tax year and the tax is due for payment on 1 December of the year following the tax year to which it relates.

Pension based on a wife's earnings

The pension is treated as earned income as opposed to investment income although at the present time there is no distinction taxwise except for wives and this too will be abolished from 6 April 1990.

A wife who has earned a private or State pension on her own contributions is currently eligible for *Wife's earnings allowance* which lets her off tax on the first £2,605 of pensions based on her own contributions plus any earnings she still has; this figure applies to the 1988–89 tax year. It is therefore possible for a wife to pay contributions on a pension obtaining tax relief, having her money accumulate without any tax and then to draw a pension which is not liable to tax as it falls within her wife's earnings tax allowance. From 1990 a wife will still get her own *personal tax allowance* which will replace her wife's earnings allowance.

From 6 April 1990 husbands and wives will be taxed completely separately so each others' pensions will not affect the amount of tax the other pays.

Why a lump sum is worth taking

Why should you take a lump sum and reduced pension instead of the full pension when you retire? You may not want to do this if you want all the proceeds to provide an income in retirement. Why not take the full pension instead?

As is so often the case, the answer is tax. *Life annuities* which you buy with your own money outside a pension scheme are taxed differently from *pension annuities* which you buy as part of a pension on retirement.

Payments made to you from an annuity which you buy yourself are partly tax free because they are considered as a return on capital and partly taxable because the rest counts as taxable income. The proportion which is tax free is larger the older you are when the life annuity starts and is larger for a man than for a woman.

Suppose a quarter of the pension fund you have accumulated on a personal pension is £25,000. You have a choice of taking it as a lump sum or as a pension. Suppose you are 65. A man of that age could obtain a pension annuity of around £3,300 a year. Assuming that your tax rate is 25%, then you pay £825 tax and after tax receive £2,475.

Instead you can take the £25,000 as a cash lump sum and buy a life annuity, for example, to give the same return with an income of £3,300. In this case though part of the life annuity, £1,750 for a man of that age, counts as a return of capital and is therefore tax free. So you pay tax on £3,300 minus £1,750 equals £1,550. At a 25% tax rate the tax on £1,550 is £387. So after tax your life annuity pays £3,300 minus £387 which comes to £2,913 a year. That is £438 a year more after tax than the pension annuity of £2,475.

In the case of a job pension, you may not be given the opportunity to shop around to get the best pension annuity rate. But if you choose the cash lump sum, you can shop around for the best life annuity rate to buy with your lump sum.

Table 5

Life annuity: proportions of lump sum used to buy the annuity which count as a return of capital

Age	Man %	Woman %	Joint[1] %
50	3.9	3.3	2.9
55	4.6	3.9	3.4
60	5.6	4.7	4.0
65	7.0	5.7	4.9
70	9.1	7.2	6.0
75	12.0	9.4	7.7

Assumes paid half-yearly in arrears without guarantee. [1]Assumes man and woman of same age.

Choosing a retirement date

You have more scope for choosing your own retirement date with private pensions than with the State scheme.

The widest flexibility is given by personal pensions which can start at any time from age 50 to 75. There is one restriction on this – contributions paid from national insurance contributions which have been switched to a personal pension because you have opted out of the State earnings related (additional) pension cannot start before age 60 for women, or 65 for men.

With a scheme run by your employer normally the employer chooses the retirement dates and these must normally be no less than 60 for men and 55 for women. The maximum normal retirement age for a job pension is 70. The retirement date for *additional voluntary contributions* must be the same as the date for the main pension scheme which they are paid in addition to. A retirement annuity can start at any time between age 60 and 75.

If you are not in a personal pension and want to retire earlier than the date of your job pension scheme this is usually possible but you will get a lower pension. Alternatively, you may be able to arrange this by arranging a transfer from the job scheme to a personal pension. You can also transfer money which is invested in a retirement annuity to a personal pension to benefit from the earlier retirement age allowed for personal pensions. There is more on transferring pensions in **Chapter 13 Changing jobs**.

If you have to retire early because of ill health, the Inland Revenue will normally agree an earlier retirement date than the normal date for your job scheme or for the limits of 50 for personal pensions and 60 for retirement annuities.

There are certain occupations which are recognised as having a traditionally earlier retirement age. However most of these were no earlier than age 50 and this list has become somewhat redundant since the introduction of 50 as the age at which personal pensions can start to be drawn by anyone.

It may seem a nice idea to retire at 50 but you are unlikely to be able to accumulate a large enough pension fund to give you a pension at that age. Even if you do, you face the problem that you have a long long time ahead of you as a pensioner and that inflation, even at relatively low rates of 3% to 5% a year, will eat into the value of your pension. **Anyone contemplating drawing a pension at age 50 should seriously consider a rising pension – or alternatively arrange to start drawing their pension in instalments between ages 50 and 75 to give a rising pension over the years**.

4
The State pension

There are two main parts to the State pension – *basic (flat rate)* and *earnings related (additional)*. For people who were employees between 1961 and 1975 there is also a small additional pension called the *graduated* pension which is based on earnings during those years.

Everyone who pays national insurance contributions is paying towards a State pension. The *State basic (flat rate) pension* has different contribution conditions from the *State earnings related (additional) pension*, commonly known as SERPS.

State basic (flat rate) pension

The State basic (flat rate) pension from April 1988 is £41.15 a week (£2,140 a year). A married man can get an additional £24.75 a week (£1,287 a year) for a non working wife or adult dependent who is not drawing her own State pension or another State benefit. Once a wife has reached pension age (over 60) this amount can be paid direct to her as her own pension. Presumably the Government does not think a wife is responsible enough to handle the money until she is over 60! There is also £8.40 a week paid for each dependent child – not very common for people over retirement age. Once you reach the age of 80, the pension is raised by a ridiculously low amount of 25p a week.

The pensions are raised each year normally from the first Monday after 6 April (which is the first day of the tax year) in line with the rise in the retail prices index in the 12 months to the previous September. The extra 25p a week for the over 80's is not.

To earn a full State basic (flat rate) pension you need to have paid national insurance contributions for most of your *working life* which is normally the period from age 16 to age 65 for a man, and from age 16 to age 60 for a woman. So your working life generally counts as 49 years for a man and 44 years for a woman.

To qualify for a full State basic (flat rate) pension you need to pay national insurance contributions (or have credits for periods of sickness or unemployment) for the whole of your working life minus five years. For a man that is normally 49 years less five which is 44 years. On the same basis for a woman it is 44 years minus five which is 39 years.

However your working life can be reduced if you qualify for *home responsibilities protection*. This mainly applies to women bringing up children but also applies if you look after someone who is disabled or very ill. Home responsibilities protection is described later in this Chapter.

If you do not have a full contributions record, your pension is paid at a reduced rate; normally with national insurance contributions paid or credited for fewer than nine or ten years you won't get any pension at all. The minimum pension is about a quarter of the normal pension.

Women who pay the reduced rate of national insurance contributions (which only applies if you had chosen to do this before 6 April 1977) do not qualify for a pension on these contributions. More on the reduced rate later in the Chapter.

If you have studied as a medical or postgraduate student say, after the age of 21 you will not get a full pension unless you paid voluntary contributions for part of your period of study or within five years after. You stop paying national insurance contributions at age 65 men, 60 women, so you can't make up later.

A husband and wife who are both earning can each build up their own State basic (flat rate) pension. If you are a working wife and the pension based on your own contributions is less than the £24.75 a week, then your State basic (flat rate) pension is raised to £24.75 a week (assuming your husband has paid enough national insurance contributions). Only if your pension, as a working wife, on your own contributions comes to more than the extra your husband would get for you as a dependent, do you receive anything extra.

If you are widowed, divorced or separated from your husband before age 60 you can use your late or former husband's national insurance contributions record towards your State basic (flat rate) pension. But to be eligible you must not remarry before you start to draw your State pension.

If you have worked abroad and paid national insurance contributions overseas, these can count towards your UK pension. This can apply to all European Community countries which are Eire, France, West Germany, Italy, Belgium, Holland, Luxemberg, Denmark, Greece, Spain and Portugal. It also applies to Gibraltar.

Other countries which have reciprocal agreements on pensions are: Australia, Austria, Bermuda, Canada,

Cyprus, Finland, Iceland, Israel, Jamaica, Jersey, Guernsey, Malta, Mauritius, New Zealand, Norway, Sweden, Switzerland, Turkey and Yugoslavia.

If you have worked abroad for long periods you may be better off drawing the pension from the foreign Government (if it allows pensions to be paid abroad) than having the contributions credited towards a UK State basic (flat rate) pension.

State earnings related (additional) pension

The State earnings related (additional) pension known as SERPS only applies to employees and company directors. If you are self-employed as a sole trader or partner you cannot belong to it. If you belong to a job pension scheme run by your employer which is *contracted-out* you are not eligible for the State earnings related (additional) pension for the period during which you were contracted out.

The State earnings related (additional) pension applies to earnings on which contributions have been paid since 6 April 1978.

People who retire in more than 12 years time – that is after 6 April 2000 – get lower pensions from their contributions than people who retire before that date.

The State earnings related (additional) pension is a percentage of the difference between the *lower earnings limit* for the tax year before the tax year in which you retire and your average earnings for years in which you have paid national insurance contributions as an employee since 6 April 1978. If you earned more than the *upper earnings limit* in any year, it is the upper limit for that year rather than your actual earnings which is used.

For the purpose of calculating the pension, your earnings for previous years, except the year immediately before the year in which you retire, are *revalued* in line with an *average earnings index*. This means each year's earnings are increased in line with how much earnings have risen throughout the country.

The result is that, broadly speaking, the value of your State earnings related (additional) pension rises in line with the average earnings index for each of the years on which your pension is based. In recent years average earnings have been increasing at about 8% a year when inflation has been rising at only 4% a year. As long as the Government doesn't change the rules, this is a plus point.

Then the lower earnings limit for the tax year before the tax year in which you retire is subtracted from the revalued earnings for each year. The result is what the DHSS calls your *surplus earnings* or more helpfully your *yearly surplus earnings*. Add all the figures up and you get your *total surplus earnings*.

How much State earnings related (additional) pension you get depends on when you retire:

● **If you are a man over 52 or a woman over 47 in 1988** you reach State retirement age (65 for a man, 60 for a woman) in about 12 years time, that is before 6 April 2000. In that case you get 1.25% (1/80th) of your *total surplus earnings* for each year you have been paying contributions as an employee since 6 April 1978. That gives a maximum State earnings related (additional) pension for 20 years contributions of 25% of your surplus earnings if you retire in 1998–99.

● **If you are a man between ages 44 and 52 or a woman between ages 39 and 47 in 1988** you retire sometime between 6 April 2000 to 5 April 2009. Your State earnings related (additional) pension is worked out as follows:

1. For contributions paid between 6 April 1978 and 5 April 1988, you multiply your surplus earnings for the years 1978–79 to 1987–88 by 25%.

2. For contributions paid from 6 April 1988 onwards the amount which you multiply your surplus earnings by for the years 1988–89 onwards depends on when you reach retirement age and is reduced by ½% for each year you retire after 6 April 2000. For example if you retire between 6 April 2000 and 5 April 2001 your State earnings related (additional) pension will be based on 24.5% of your surplus earnings for the years 1988–89 to 1999–2000; if you retire in 2001–2002 it will be based on 24% of your surplus earnings from 1988–89 to 2000–2001 and so on.

3. Having multiplied surplus earnings by the appropriate percentage, you then add up the two separate calculations and divide by the total number of years (inclusive) from 1978–79 to the tax year before the one in which you reach retirement age.

● **If you are a man under age 44 or a woman under age 39 now** you retire on or after 6 April 2009. Your State earnings related (additional) pension is worked out as follows:

1. For contributions paid between 6 April 1978 and 5 April 1988, you multiply your surplus earnings for the years 1978–79 to 1987–88 by 25%.

2. For contributions paid from 6 April 1988 onwards you multiply your surplus earnings for the years 1988–89 onward by 20%.

3. Having multiplied your surplus earnings by the appropriate percentage, you add the two separate calculations together. Then divide by the total number of years (inclusive) from 1978–79 to the tax year before the one when you reach retirement age.

So far you may have found the explanation of the State earnings related (additional) pension rather heavy going. It is more easily explained by an example. But if you have had enough, you can obtain an estimate of what your State earnings related (additional) pension is likely to be from the Government. Phone the DHSS enquiry office on 0800-666-555 (the offices are only open during normal working hours and there is no charge for the call) and ask them to send you a copy of leaflet *NP38 Your Future Pension*. The leaflet has a form for you to send off to obtain the estimate. If you are an employer and want a set for all your employees there is an employer's enquiry number 0800-393-539. If these numbers are engaged or don't answer try your local DHSS office. You may also be able to get this leaflet at Citizens' Advice Bureaux and Post Offices.

An example

It is easier to understand the worth of the State earnings related (additional) pension if you look at an example where all the figures are in today's values and prices. The actual amount you get when you retire will be much more – but it will be worth about the same in today's money.

Suppose you are earning £10,000 a year as an employee. And you have been earning at that level as an employee in today's money for many years. Had this been the case your *revalued earnings* will also be £10,000 for every year.

Suppose you retire on March 31 1999. That is during the 1998–99 tax year (which runs from 6 April 1998 to 5 April 1999.)

Assume you have paid national insurance contributions as an employee and that the lower earnings limit in the tax year before the tax year in which you retire is worth the same as the current year's one of £2,132. So your *yearly surplus earnings*, the difference between your *revalued earnings* and the *lower earnings limit*, is £10,000 minus £2,132 equals £7,868.

One eightieth (1.25%) of your surplus earnings of £7,868 is £98.35 which is the pension you have earned for one year's contributions. So if you retire towards the end of 1998–99 you can get an State earnings related (additional) pension of about 20/80ths or 25% which is £1,967 in today's money.

If you earn more than the *upper earnings limit* your yearly surplus earnings is the difference between the lower earnings limit and the upper earnings limit. Using the current limits of £2,132 and £15,860 that is £13,728. One eightieth (1.25%) of that is £171.60 and 20/80ths (25%) give a pension of £3,432 a year, again in today's money.

A husband and wife can each earn these pensions on their own earnings. And they are paid in addition to the State basic (flat rate) pension.

If you read the explanation above, you will know that working out an example of what your pension will be if you are younger than 52 (men), 47 (women), is even more complex. The table on page 50 shows examples in today's money of different earnings levels and what the State earnings related (additional) pension could be. It assumes that your earnings stay at the figures given in today's money and that average earnings and prices rise at the same level.

If you reckon your earnings will grow in *real* terms ie in 10 years time you reckon you will be earning £12,000 a year in today's money compared with £10,000 a year now, then you can use a combination of the figures.

For example if you retire in 1998–99 and you reckon part of your working life will be at earnings of £10,000 a year in today's money and part at £12,000, look up the figure in the table for each. For £10,000 earnings the pension you might get is £1,967 a year and at £12,000 it is £2,467. So your pension could be between £1,967 and £2,467.

Home responsibilities protection

To earn a full State pension you need to have paid national insurance contributions for most of your *working life* which is normally the period from age 16 to age 65 for a man, and to age 60 for a woman. Your working life generally counts as 49 years for a man and 44 years for a woman.

However your working life can be reduced if you qualify for *home responsibilities protection*. This mainly applies if you aren't working because you are bringing up children and also if you look after someone who is disabled or very ill. Home responsibilities protection can raise the State basic (flat rate) pension and the Government proposes to extend the protection to the State earnings related (additional) pension. Both men and women are eligible.

For the State basic (flat rate) pension The working life used to work out your pension is normally 49 years for a man and 44 for a woman, less 5 years in both cases. This can be further reduced for each full tax year during which you received home responsibilities protection.

Suppose you spend 13 full tax years (after 6 April 1978 when this protection first started) not earning, or earning less than the lower earnings limit for national insurance contributions in each of the years. If you are a woman in this position your 'working life' would otherwise normally be 44 years less 5 years. The home responsibilities

Table 6

How much State earnings related (additional) pension yc
might get a year when you retire measured in today's mone

Tax year you reach retirement age	Your age in 1988 Man	Woman	Your current yearly earnings before tax and deductions £6,000 £	£10,000 £	£15,860[1] £	Number of years in scheme
1988–89	65	60	484	984	1716	10
1989–90	64	59	532	1082	1888	11
1990–91	63	58	580	1180	2059	12
1991–92	62	57	296	1279	2231	13
1992–93	61	56	677	1377	2402	14
1993–94	60	55	725	1475	2574	15
1994–95	59	54	774	1574	2746	16
1995–96	58	53	822	1672	2917	17
1996–97	57	52	870	1770	3089	18
1997–98	56	51	919	1869	3260	19
1998–99	55	50	967	1967	3432	20
1999–2000	54	49	967	1967	3432	21
2000–01	53	48	956	1946	3395	22
2001–02	52	47	945	1923	3354	23
2002–03	51	46	933	1898	3312	24
2003–04	50	45	921	1873	3267	25
2004–05	49	44	907	1846	3221	26
2005–06	48	43	894	1818	3173	27
2006–07	47	42	880	1790	3123	28
2007–08	46	41	866	1761	3072	29
2008–09	45	40	851	1731	3020	30
2009–10	44	39	836	1701	2967	31
2010–11	43	38	834	1697	2960	32
2011–12	42	37	832	1693	2954	33
2012–13	41	36	830	1689	2947	34

able 6 continued

x year u reach tirement e	Your age in 1988 Man	Woman	Your current yearly earnings before tax and deductions			Number of years in scheme
			£6,000 £	£10,000 £	£15,860[1] £	
)13–14	40	35	829	1686	2942	35
)14–15	39	34	827	1683	2936	36
)15–16	38	33	826	1680	2931	37
)16–17	37	32	824	1677	2926	38
)17–18	36	31	823	1674	2922	39
)18–19	35	30	822	1672	2917	40

above.

protection reduces it by 13 years to 31 years less four years. To get the full State pension you therefore need only have paid contributions for 27 years against 39 years for a woman who has not received home responsibilities protection.

You can get the full State basic (flat rate) pension if the reduced number of qualifying years in your working life (after taking account of your home responsibilities years) is at least 20 or more.

Home responsibilities protection can be taken to mean that you need work for only five years of your life paying national insurance contributions (or getting credits for periods of sickness or unemployment) and you can receive some State basic (flat rate) pension (around 25% of the basic rate). But remember if you are a married woman living with your husband you may not actually get any extra money because you can get a pension based on your husband's contributions and you can only get the larger one, not both; this was explained earlier in this Chapter.

For the State earning related (additional) pension At the moment home responsibilities protection only affects the State basic (flat rate) pension and not the

State earnings related (additional) pension. But if you retire after 6 April 1999 it will also help with your State earnings related (additional) pension.

When working out your State earnings related (additional) pension, you divide your revalued earnings by the number of years from 1978–79, or when you were 16 if later, to your retirement age. With home responsibilities protection you will probably be able to deduct the years of protection, say 13, from the total years, say 33 to reduce the period to as low as 20 years. The details of how this protection will work have not yet been finalised.

The reduced rate of national insurance

If before 6 April 1977 you were a married woman who was then paying the *reduced rate* of national insurance and, broadly speaking, you continued working without a break of more than two years since 6 April 1977, you are allowed to continue to pay at the reduced rate.

You are not earning yourself any State pension while you remain on the reduced rate. You have the right to choose to pay the full rate of national insurance but you might consider putting the contributions into a personal pension instead. However if you are planning to do that you also might consider paying the full rate of national insurance and then *contracting-out*.

What you pay for a State pension

There are four classes of national insurance contributions:

Class 1 is paid by employees and company directors and depends on your earnings. There is a lower earnings limit, £41 a week for 1988–89, and if you earn less than this you do not have to pay contributions but you do not then notch up any rights to a pension (or unemployment, sickness or

maternity benefit). There are three Class 1 types:
● *Not contracted-out* which for ease of understanding I shall sometimes refer to as 'contracted-in'.
● *Contracted-out* which gives no rights to SERPS.
● *Reduced rate* for certain married women and widows referred to above. This gives no rights to any pension.

Class 2 is a flat rate contribution paid by the self-employed, sole traders and partners. This is a fixed weekly amount (which you can pay in four weekly amounts) and does not depend on income. For 1988–89 the rate is £4.05 a week. For women who hold a certificate entitling them to the *reduced rate*, no contributions are payable.

Class 3 is a flat rate which you can pay voluntarily if you want to save towards a State basic (flat rate) pension and are not given credits (in effect free contributions when you are sick or unemployed). You might want to pay Class 3 if your earnings are too low to pay Class 1. For 1988–89 the rate is £3.95 a week. More details are given in a free DHSS leaflet National Insurance Voluntary Contributions NI 42.

Class 4 contributions are profit related and are paid by the self-employed. They give no benefits. The State pension for the self-employed depends entirely on Class 2 contributions. For 1988–89 Class 4 contributions are 6.3% of profits between £4,750 a year and £15,860 a year.

If you change from being employed to self-employed, your pension is based on a mixture of your contributions of either type. You can ask your local DHSS office for a statement of your contributions to date. You may not find it so easy to discover which is the office for your area and you may be unlucky like me and not receive a reply! The DHSS has been known to have incorrect records so if you keep all your old pay slips, or details of when you paid if you are self-employed, until you retire you can challenge them if they say you have not paid enough contributions.

Table 7
National insurance contributions for employees 1988–89

Total yearly earnings £	Weekly earnings £	Contracted-in rate %	Contracted-out rate[1] %	Reduc rate[2] %
2,132 to 3,639	41 to 69	5	3	3.85
3,640 to 5,459	70 to 104	7	5	3.85
5,460 to 8,059	105 to 154	9	7	3.85
8,060 to 15,860	155 to 305	9	7	3.85
Over £15,860 on first £15,860	Over £305 on first £305	9	7	3.85

[1]These rates apply to earnings between £41 and £305. The first £41 a week are at the contracted- rate. [2]For married women and widows who paid this rate before 1977 and have not since lost the ri to pay at this rate.

Retirement age

State pensions can only be paid from age 65 for men or age 60 for women. If you want to retire early you can't get your State pension earlier. If you want to retire later you can defer your State pension for up to five years to 70 for a man or 65 for a woman.

In return the pension is raised by 7.5% a year simple interest (that means you get a maximum increase of 37.5%). The increase is based on the level of pension when you eventually retire, not the level when you were 65 or 60.

It is well worth defering your retirement if you continue to earn money from a job or self-employment or receive royalties as your State pension will be reduced by the *earnings rule* if your earnings are more than £75 a week (£3,900 a year) currently or the earnings of a wife or adult dependent are normally more than £32.75 a week (£1,703 a year). In calculating the 'earnings' for the purpose of the

Table 8

How much you pay in national insurance 1988–89

Weekly earnings	Amount paid Contracted-in[1] £	out £	Yearly earnings £ £	Amount paid Contracted-in[1]	out
Employee					
0	Nil	Nil	2,000	Nil	Nil
5	3.25	2.77	3,500	175	148
0	7.00	5.82	5,000	350	293
0	13.50	11.32	8,000	720	603
0	18.00	14.82	10,000	900	743
0	27.00	21.82	15,000	1,350	1,093

Weekly profit	Amount paid £	Yearly profit £	Amount paid £
Self-employed			
	Nil	2,000	Nil
to 91	4.05	5,000	226
0	7.75	8,000	415
0	10.89	10,000	541
0	17.19	15,000	856

Contracted-in means not contracted-out

earnings rule (but not for tax) you can deduct a few expenses, the most widely applicable being the cost of travelling to and from work.

What you might get from the State

Most people can expect to get something close to the full basic retirement pension. If you are single you can get:
● The basic pension of £2,140 a year.

● A graduated pension of from 5.4p a week to £4.64 a
week for men or to £3.88 a week for women (£2.80 a year
to £241 a year for men or to £202 a year for women) if you
were employed between 1961 and 1975.

● If you are an employee contributing towards the State
earnings related (additional) pension, a State earnings
related (additional) pension (depending on your earnings)
of between £484 a year on earnings averaging £6,000 a
year after 10 years in the scheme to £3,432 a year on
earnings averaging £15,860 or over a year after 20 years
in the scheme.

If you are married, husband and wife can each get the
above pensions. If one of the spouses is not entitled to any
basic pension or a small one, but the other has a full basic
pension, then there is a spouse's pension of £24.75 a week
(£1,287 a year).

So it is possible for a man whose wife has no State
pension on her own contributions to draw a pension of
£7,100 a year from the State. A woman (without an adult
dependent) can get a maximum of £5,774.

And a couple who have both worked for most of their
adult lives and have each been on high earnings worth
£15,860 or more in today's money since 1978 could
between them get State pensions worth £11,587 a year
which is 36½% of their total earnings of £31,720.

For people who retire after 1999 this maximum gradually reduces year by year.

These pensions are in today's values but because the
State pension rises each year in line with the retail prices
index, you can be reasonably confident that the pension
you actually receive when you retire is worth the same in
the future as it does in today's money.

Free DHSS leaflets on State pensions

The following leaflets are relevent to State pensions. You can get them from a local office of the Department of Health and Social Security and usually from Citizens' Advice Bureaux. A few may be found in main Post Offices.

NP 12   School leavers and students: what you pay and what you get

NP 16   NI contributions for people working in the UK for embassies, consulates or other overseas employees

NP 18   Class 4 National Insurance contributions

NP 23   Employer's guide to occupational pension schemes and contracting out

NP 27   Looking after someone at home? How to protect your pension

NP 28   More than one job? Class 1 Contributions

NP 32   Your retirement pension

NP 32A Your retirement pension if you are widowed or divorced

NP 32B Retirement benefits for married women

NP 36   Your benefit as a widow

NP 38   Your future pension

NP 39   Your Additional Pension statement

NI 1   National insurance choices for a married woman

NI 27A People with small earnings from self-employment

NI 35   National insurance for company directors

NI 38   Social security abroad

NI 39   National insurance and contract of service

NI 40   National insurance for employees

NI 41 National insurance guide for the self-employed
NI 42 National insurance voluntary contributions
NI 47 National insurance for share fishermen
NI 48 National insurance – unpaid and late paid contributions
NI 50 National insurance guide for war pensioners
NI 51 National insurance for widows
NI 92 Earning extra pension by cancelling retirement
NI 95 National insurance for divorced women
NI 105 Retirement pensions and widows benefits: payment direct into bank or building society accounts
NI 125 Training for future employment and your national insurance record
NI 132 National insurance for people working abroad
NI 192 National insurance for agencies and people finding work through agencies
NI 196 Social security benefit rates and earnings rules
NI 208 National insurance rates
NI 222 National insurance for examiners and part time lecturers, teachers and instructors
NI 230 Unemployment benefit and your occupational pension
NI 255 Class 2 and Class 3 National insurance contributions: direct debit the easy way to pay!
NI 256 National insurance: abolition of the married woman's half test
NI 258 National insurance: abolition of the married woman's 156 test

5
If you are an employee without a pension

If you work for someone else and your job doesn't have a pension with it, you are eligible to contribute to a personal pension. You would be wise to contribute as much as you can afford. But it may also be worth your while to switch some of your national insurance contributions into a personal pension and opt out of the *State earnings related (additional) pension*. This option has only become available in 1988 and as it coincides with a reduction in the benefits payable from future contributions to the State earnings related scheme, it is something you should consider.

You now have the right to choose to opt out of the State earnings related pension called The *Additional Pension* by the Government and otherwise known as *SERPS*. In this book it is called the State earnings related (additional) pension.

Should you leave the State earnings related (additional) pension?

Originally the Government wanted to abolish the State earnings related (additional) pension. But because of the outcry against the decision by trade unionists and others it decided instead to gradually reduce the benefits.

Details of the changes which came into effect from 6 April 1988 are given in **Chapter 3 How pensions work**. In summary, contributions you made up to 6 April 1988 for the past ten years (when the scheme was introduced) are normally unaffected. The pension you get based on these will normally be paid when you retire on the original basis. Benefits in respect of contributions made from 6 April 1988 build up at a lower rate – but you get a better deal the older you are now.

Your decision on whether to opt out of the State earnings related (additional) pension depends mainly on your age now and whether you are a man or a woman.

It is generally agreed that if in 1988 you are a man under age 46 or a woman under age 41 you are better off opting out of the State earnings related (additional) pension and you should backdate your choice for the 1987–88 tax year too.

If you are age 53 or over for men or age 48 or over for women you are not affected by the change in the basis of the State earnings related (additional) pension and are better off staying in the State earnings related (additional) pension. Remember that you can still take out a separate personal pension even if you remain in the State scheme.

If you are aged from 46 to 53 for men and 41 to 48 for women you can probably do better by opting out of the State earnings related (additional) pension but whether you should opt out depends on how well you think the investments in your personal pension fund will grow. The more optimistic you are about this and the closer you are to the lower age limits, the more likely you should be to choose to opt out of the State scheme.

You can change your mind in future years and contract back in to the State earnings related (additional) pension if circumstances change.

Comparing what you get from the State

You can get an estimate of what you would get out of the State earnings related (additional) pension if you stayed in from the DHSS. Ideally you should then be able to ask a pensions company to give you an estimate of how much pension you can expect to have at retirement age if you opt out of the State earnings related scheme. You can then compare the figures and make your decision. Several pensions companies have prepared ready reckoners which show the estimated profit or loss you make at different current earnings if you decide to leave the State earnings related pension. The problem is ensuring that the estimates are comparable – and are based on the same assumptions.

Your future pension NP38 is an official leaflet which you can get by phoning the DHSS on 0800-666-555 (the phone call is free). Unfortunately you may find the number is engaged or you get a recorded message saying "The service is temporarily out of action, please phone again later." You can also get the leaflet from local DHSS offices, Citizens Advice Bureaux and possibly Post Offices.

When you get the leaflet, complete the tear-off form which is part of it, add your national insurance number (if you don't have it to hand ask the wages department at work) and send it off to the address on the form.

After a few weeks – or possibly longer if as a result of the extensive publicity which the Government is carrying out millions of others do the same – you get back a computer typed personally addressed letter headed 'About your additional pension' which comes with a leaflet *NP39 A fact sheet about your additional pension statement.* Parts of the fact sheet are very difficult to understand because the rules are very complex. The letter gives you three separate figures:

1. How much is your Additional Pension worth at the moment? 'Additional Pension' is what the Government calls the State earnings related pension. This information is not much use unless you are about to retire shortly in which case you should not be contemplating opting out of this scheme. My letter said 'You might like to think of it as the amount of Additional Pension you would get when you are 65 if you had stopped paying into the scheme on 5 April 1987.'

If there has been some mistake in your contributions record – for instance your employer or a previous employer has not paid your contributions over to the DHSS, or they have been recorded wrongly, you won't be able to tell from this Statement as it does not tell you when you paid contributions. If you want to check up that your contributions record is correct, you have to write to your local DHSS office asking for a statement of your contributions to date.

The letter about the additional pension probably does not include anything you have paid since the beginning of the tax year before the one in which you receive the Statement – ie 5 April 1987. But it tells you in the first paragraph what period of contributions are covered.

2. How much will your Additional Pension be when you are 65 for a man, 60 for a woman. This assumes you earn broadly the same as you are now ie you do not get promotion or demotion, that you do not have periods of unemployment and that you continue to be an employee. If you become self-employed the estimate will not be correct. However if you stop work to look after children or a disabled person you will normally not lose out seriously for the missed years (more on this in **Chapter 4** under the heading *Home responsibilities protection*). This estimate is also in today's money.

3. How much will it be if your pay rises faster than inflation? This assumes that your earnings rise by 1.5% a year more than the rate of increase of prices. Again the estimate is to age 65 for men and 60 for women. For instance if the retail prices index rises by 4% a year from now until your retirement age, the estimate assumes that your earnings go up by 5.5% a year. The estimate is in today's money. It is this third estimate which is the most useful for you when deciding whether to opt out of the State earnings related (additional) pension. If you are already earning more than the *upper earnings limit* (£15,860 in 1988–89) this estimate is the same as the second estimate as you cannot earn extra State earnings related (additional) pension from pay increases over the limit.

4. How will the years when you 'contracted-out' affect it? If you have been in an employer's contracted-out pension then your State earnings related (additional) pension is reduced. If this applies the amount of the reduction is shown. If you are already contracted-out, of course, you cannot contract-out again, so you need agonise no further on that decision.

Comparing with a personal pension

Having obtained your estimate of what you might get by staying in the State earnings related (additional) pension you need to ask a pensions company to give you an estimate on the same basis.

The newly introduced Financial Services Act has brought in a wad of complex rules aimed at standardising the way in which illustrations of future benefits of these policies are given. In some respects these rules are an improvement on the previous position:

● They force all pensions companies to base projections for personal pensions on common rates of return.

● In the case of projections for contributions switched from the State earnings related (additional) pension to a personal pension, they force companies to give the projections using *real rates of return* which means the projections you should get will be comparable with the estimate you can get from the DHSS.

The main drawback with the new rules is that they are absolutely useless in helping you choose a pensions company as every company must assume it makes the same basic charges and gives the same basic benefits on its policies. So unless you ask for some extras, all companies will give you the same projected pension. There is more on this in **Chapter 12 Which pension company?**

The other drawback is that *deposit based personal pensions*, that is pensions offered by building societies or banks as an investment in their own interest paying deposits are not covered by the Financial Services Act and do not have to make illustrations on this basis. However it is possible that they will give illustrations assuming a *real rate of return* voluntarily if they give you a pensions illustration based on opting out of the State earnings related (additional) pension.

Here are two checklists summarising the points in favour and against switching out of the State earnings related (additional) pension scheme.

In favour of opting out

● A chance to benefit from investment growth on your money and get a larger pension.

● Extra contributions can be used to generate a cash lump sum with tax relief, tax exemption and no tax when you take it.

● You depend on private enterprise rather than the State.

● Tax relief on part of your own national insurance contributions, the *rebate*, which is redirected into a personal pension. You don't get this tax relief otherwise.

● An extra *incentive* payment made by the Government to your pension for up to six years.

● There is a danger that if earnings rises in general continue to exceed price rises by a wide margin that the Government will link the accumulation of the State earnings related (additional) pension to prices instead of earnings (or to prices plus a fixed margin of say 1.5% which is the assumption in its Additional Pension Statement). That would give you a relatively lower State pension when you retire.

In favour of staying in

● The pension is guaranteed as a proportion of your average earnings (or part of them if you earn more than the higher earnings limit).

● The pension is index-linked with average earnings generally as it accumulates so you are protected against inflation and so long as earnings rise by more than prices, you will do better than inflation.

● No risk of losing money if stock market crashes or investment managers suffer from poor luck or judgement.

● The pension is guaranteed by the Government – so there is no worry about the pension company getting into trouble even though pension companies are usually covered by compensation schemes of between 75% and 90% of benefits.

● Your pension depends on the level of the *lower*

earnings limit in the tax year before the year in which you retire (see **Chapter 4 The State pension**). This limit is linked to the value of the State basic pension which currently is linked to rises in prices. If the lower earnings limit falls relative to average earnings then if you don't leave the State earnings related (additional) pension, your State earnings related (additional) pension will be higher than can be estimated now. At present average earnings rises are 8% a year compared with price rises of around 4% a year. That means earnings are rising considerably faster than prices. As the Government estimate described in this Chapter assumes earnings rise by only 1.5% a year more than prices, that could considerably undervalue your pension if you are a long way from retirement. But you may be clobbered if the Government changes the rules, see the last point in the list in favour of opting out.

Minimum contribution personal pension

You might expect the personal pension you have chosen to contract-out of the State earnings related (additional) pension with, to be an ordinary personal pension. Unfortunately that is not the case. For reasons which are not fully clear the Government has imposed tighter restrictions on pensions that are built up with your national insurance *rebate* and *incentive* than it does on other personal pensions. How much this rebate and incentive come to is explained later in this Chapter.

Retirement age

If you are thinking of retiring at 50 with a personal pension from your national insurance rebate, forget it. You cannot draw this type of personal pension before the

State retirement age, currently age 65 for a man and 60 for a woman. Unlike a personal pension you cannot take it earlier although you can take it later up to age 75. It does not allow for early retirement from age 50 which other personal pensions can.

Lump sum

There is no lump sum available from this type of pension. So you can't boost your pension in the way explained in **Chapter 3 How pensions work** by using the lump sum to buy a life annuity.

Pension annuity

When you want to start drawing a personal pension at retirement age you have to buy a pension annuity from a life insurance company – or get one from the life company you have been saving towards your pension with. With a personal pension derived from your national insurance contributions rebate this pension annuity must be one which rises by 3% a year (or by the retail prices index if that is less than 3% a year). It must also be one which pays a pension to your wife or husband after you die of at least half the amount payable to you.

Although these conditions are quite reasonable, they have the effect of considerably reducing the pension you get at the outset by around one third compared with the situation if you provided no protection for your spouse or against inflation. If you and your wife are in poor health at retirement age for instance, you would not want to cut your standard of living now in return for rises in a future you might not be around to enjoy.

Pension annuities used on this type of contracted-out personal pension must be unisex – that is men and women of the same age must be given the same pension rate.

Normally women get a lower pension because they live longer. This has the effect of making these contracted-out personal pensions less attractive to men and more attractive to women.

More than the minimum

These restrictive rules on contracted-out personal pensions apply to the pension which you receive as a result of the investment of your national insurance rebate and incentive. The restrictions do not have to apply to the extra amount you pay over and above the redirection of the rebate of national insurance contributions and the incentive.

However that is at the discretion of the pension company. If you only want to pay a small amount in addition to the redirected national insurance contributions and incentive you may find the pensions company insists that these too are treated on the same terms as the contracted-out part of your pension (eg retirement not before State ages, and no lump sum). It is likely that the pensions company will expect you to pay at least its normal minimum contribution – say £20 a month or £200 a year – as well as what you are putting in as the contracted-out pension. You should make sure of this point before you commit yourself.

Saving towards a tax free lump sum

There can be a rather good deal if you choose to contract-out of the State earnings related (additional) pension *and* contribute extra yourself. Provided the pensions company agrees, the whole of the amount you pay extra (provided it is no more than about 33% of what is going into your fund from the national insurance rebate and the incentive) can be towards a tax free lump sum on retirement.

While there are restrictions on how the proceeds of your personal pension earned on your national insurance rebate and incentive are paid, the fund which accumulates for you from your national insurance contributions counts as part of any larger fund which you accumulate as a personal pension with your own contributions.

On retirement you can take 25% of your fund as a tax free lump sum on any personal pension. The same applies to a fund built up partly out of redirected national insurance contributions provided you have contributed at least 33% extra. If you contribute 10% extra, the maximum lump sum is about 9% of your pension fund; if you contribute 20% extra, it is about 17%.

If you earn less than £15,860 in 1988–89 the DHSS pays 8.47% of your earnings less the lower earnings limit of £2,132 into a personal pension (for how this 8.47% is made up see later in this Chapter). So if you are earning £10,000 this year £10,000 minus £2,132 equals £7,868. And 8.47% of £7,868 is £666.42.

Now if you pay an extra contribution of 33% of your rebate and incentive – in this example it would be 33% of £666.42 which is £219.92 a year – then all that money can be used to go towards a tax free lump sum when you retire provided the pensions company agrees.

If you earn £15,860 or more then the DHSS pays 8.47% of the difference between the lower and upper earnings limit (ie 8.47% of £13,728 for 1988–89). That is £1,162.76. So you can pay a maximum extra contribution of £383.71 a year.

Your extra contributions get full tax relief, grow tax free, and when you retire you can take all the proceeds back tax free as a lump sum. And if you wish to convert them into a pension you can take advantage of the normally lower tax paid on the income from life annuities described in **Chapter 3 How pensions work**. But if your contributions are more than 33% of the amount paid by

the DHSS to your personal pension then only 25% of your
total fund can be towards a lump sum, the rest must be
towards a pension.

How opting out works

The official phrase is to *contract-out* of the State earnings
related (additional) pension. If you contract-out, you have
to go into a personal pension instead and this is sometimes
called the *contracted-out personal pension* or the *minimum contribution personal pension* or the *protected rights
pension* or the *appropriate personal pension*.

If you decide to opt out, part of your national insurance
contributions and your employer's national insurance
contributions is paid by the Department of Health and
Social Security (DHSS) to a personal pension scheme
which you choose. These contributions are known as the
rebate. The DHSS also makes an *incentive* payment into
your personal pension which amounts to an additional 2%
a year on part of your earnings. This incentive payment
will continue until 5 April 1993 (ie for up to six years).
You are also allowed *tax relief* on your part of the national
insurance rebate but not on the incentive or your
employer's contributions.

Although you and your employer pay your national
insurance contributions weekly or monthly, the DHSS
does not pay the money to the pension company until
later. It pays over the money for the whole year about
three months (or more) after the end of the tax year in
which the contributions are made. For example contributions you make from 6 April 1988 to 5 April 1989 will not
be paid to the pension company until July 1989 or later.
So you lose out on interest and growth on your money.

But you can decide to back date your choice to opt out of
the State earnings related (additional) pension to the
beginning of the 1987–88 tax year ie until 6 April 1987

provided you make the choice before 6 April 1989.

The actual amounts of national insurance contributions and incentive which are paid to a personal pension by the DHSS depend on your earnings. They are worked out according to the earnings limits for State national insurance contributions for employees.

For the 1988–89 tax year the *lower earnings limit* is £2,132 a year (£41 a week) and the *upper earnings limit* is £15,860 a year (£305 a week). These limits rise in line with rises in the retail prices index.

For the 1987–88 tax year the *lower earnings limit* was £2,028 a year (£39 a week) and the *upper earnings limit* was £15,340 a year (£295 a week).

National insurance contributions which are paid by the DHSS to a personal pension when you opt out of the State earnings related scheme are based on percentages of the difference between the lower earnings limit and your earnings, or if you are above the higher limit, on the difference between the two limits.

For example if you earn £10,000 a year this tax year, then the contributions are based on a percentage of the difference between the lower earnings limit, £2,132, and your earnings of £10,000. Subtract the lower earnings limit £2,132 from your earnings of £10,000 and you get £7,868. That is the band of earnings on which the various contracted-out national insurance contributions and the incentive are worked out on.

The rebate of national insurance contributions for the 1988–89 tax year with figures for the 1987–88 tax year in brackets is as follows: employers 3.8% (4.1%), employees 2% (2.15%).

The incentive paid to a personal pension if you opt out of the State earnings related (additional) pension is 2% for each of the six tax years from 1987–88 to 1993–94.

Tax relief at the basic rate is given on your own national insurance contributions which are paid into a personal pension but not on the employer's contributions nor on the incentive. Your own national insurance contributions rebate which is paid to a personal pension is deemed to be paid after deduction of tax at the basic rate. This is an advantage to you and gives better tax relief.

As the rebate is deemed to be after deduction of basic rate tax, the actual amount is *grossed up* to find the before tax amount. Here is an example of how it works for the 1988–89 tax year which started on 6 April 1988.

Suppose your rebate of national insurance is £100. With the basic rate of tax at 25%, the grossed up rate is:

£100 ÷ ·75 = £133.33

So the tax relief is 25% of £133.33 which is £33.33 for each £100 of the rebate rather than £25 if they were not grossed up.

For the last tax year 1987–88 when the basic rate of tax was 27% the grossed up rate for each £100 of rebate was:

£100 ÷ ·73 = £136.99

The DHSS claims the basic rate tax relief back from the Inland Revenue and hands it over to the pensions company. For 1988–89 the basic tax relief amounts to 0.67% (for 1987–88 it was 0.8%).

Total payment made to your personal pension by the DHSS if you opt out of the State earnings related (additional) pension for 1988–89 consists of:
● The rebate of 3.8% for employers
● The rebate of 2% for employees national insurance
● 2% incentive
● 0.67% basic tax relief
● Making a total of 8.47%.
  For 1987–88 it consists of:
● The rebate of 4.1% for employers
● The rebate of 2.15% for employees

- The 2% incentive
- 0.8% basic tax relief
- Making a total of 9.05%.

In all cases this is on the difference between the lower earnings limit and your earnings, or if you earn the upper earnings limit or above, the difference between the upper and the lower earnings limit.

Higher rate taxpayers get tax relief at the higher rates which they can get in a tax assessment or Notice of Coding. For 1988–89 the tax relief on the rebate is generally worth 0.4% of the difference between the lower and upper earnings limits. For 1987–88 it depends on the rate of higher rate tax applicable. You have to claim the difference between the basic and the higher rate of tax yourself if you are eligible.

An example of opting out

Let's summarise what is being invested for you with a complete example. Suppose you are earning £10,000 a year now and earned £9,500 last year. Examples are also given if you earn £15,860 or more in 1988–89 or earned £15,340 or more in 1987–88.

For this year 1988–89

We worked out above that the difference between earnings of £10,000 and the lower earnings limit this year (1988–89) is £7,868. So if you choose to opt out of the State earnings related (additional) pension, the rebate which the DHSS will pay into your personal pension is 3.8% for your employer's contribution plus 2% for your own contribution plus the incentive of 2%, plus tax relief of .67% which makes a total of 8.47% which multiplied by £7,868 comes to £666.42. So you have £666.42 credited to your personal pension plan.

If you earn £15,860 or over then your national insurance rebate and incentive is based on the difference between the lower earnings limit (£2,132) and the higher earnings limit (£15,860) which is £13,728. So your rebate for national insurance if you choose to opt out this year is 3.8% for your employer's contribution plus 2% for your own contribution plus the incentive of 2% plus tax relief of 0.67% which makes a total 8.47% of £13,728 which is £1,162.76. So you have £1,162.76 credited to your personal pension plan.

For last year 1987–88

Suppose you earned £9,500 in the last tax year which ended on 5 April 1988. The lower earnings limit for that year was £2,028. Subtract that from your earnings of £9,500 and you get £7,472.

So your rebate for national insurance if you decide to opt out for last year as well is 4.1% for your employer's contribution plus 2.15% for your own contribution plus the incentive of 2% plus tax relief of 0.8% which makes a total of 9.05% of £7,472 which is £676.22. So your personal pension is credited with £676.22.

If you were earning £15,340 or more in 1987–88 then your national insurance rebate and incentive was based on the difference between the lower earnings limit for that year (£2,028) and the higher earnings limit (£15,340). Subtract one from the other and you get £13,312. So if you decide to opt out for last year as well, your rebate for national insurance is 4.1% for your employer's contribution plus 2.15% for your own contribution plus the incentive of 2% plus tax relief of 0.8% which makes a total 9.05% of £13,312 which comes to £1,204.74. So your personal pension is credited with £1,204.74.

What it adds up to

By choosing to opt out of the State earnings related (additional) pension if you are on £10,000 this year and £9,500 last year, you create a pension fund for yourself worth £676.22 from last year plus £666.42 for 1988–89 which comes to a total of £1,342.64 at a cost to you over two years of £318.01 in national insurance contributions.

If your earnings are £15,860 or more for 1988–89 and were £15,360 or more last year you will create a fund worth £2,329.39 at a cost to you over two years of £560.77 in national insurance contributions. If you are a higher rate taxpayer you get higher rate tax relief on your own national insurance contributions which cuts the cost in 1988–89 in this example by another £54.91; the reduction in 1987–88 depends on the rate of tax you paid.

It sound excellent but before you go ahead you must check what you are getting for it and what you are giving up.

How to leave the State earnings related pension

You can only opt out of the State earnings related (additional) pension if you join another pension scheme instead. If your employer does not intend to introduce a pension scheme with your job, your only choice is through a personal pension.

You must first decide which pensions company you want to put your pension with. To make this choice you need to read **Chapter 8 How your money grows** and **Chapter 12 Which pensions company**. Once you have decided this, you just fill in a form which the pensions company will give you.

A new job pension

If your employer decides to introduce a new job pension scheme for all employees or for a few individuals including yourself you have to decide whether you want to join your employer's new pension scheme or do your own thing. The considerations are discussed in **Chapter 6 If you are already in a job pension**. Some more detailed aspects are also covered from your employer's point of view in **Chapter 11 If you employ people** which you should read too if you want to know why he has introduced the type of scheme he has chosen. What is in his best interests is not necessarily in your own.

Do nothing

If you decide not to join an employer's pension you can take a personal pension, or even stay out of both and just rely on the State earnings related (additional) pension. Job pensions are no longer compulsory, neither do you have to go into a personal pension if you don't want to. However if you are under age 46 for a man or under age 41 for a woman, you are almost certainly better off opting out of the State earnings related (additional) pension into a personal pension even if you don't make any extra contributions.

6
If you are already in a job pension

A pension with your job can be a very good deal, especially if you are a long serving employee working for an old established organisation or you work in the public sector in the civil service, the health service, a local authority or a nationalised industry like British Rail or British Coal.

But if you are young and don't expect to stay with your company for long, you could be better off making your own arrangements and not belonging to a job pension scheme at all. That is because when you leave a job pension, the amount you can take with you, your *transfer* value, may not be any more than the amount you have paid as contributions yourself without interest.

What do you belong to

Before you do anything it is essential to find out how your job pension scheme actually works – and what it offers. Large organisations have special Pensions Departments; at other firms it will be the Personnel Department which deals with pensions, and with some companies it will be Wages or Accounts. It is a legal requirement that the pension scheme has a booklet available which gives full details of the job pension scheme and how to work out what you are entitled to from the pension scheme. You should also be given an *annual report* each year showing how the pension fund investments are performing. You are also entitled to an annual *benefit statement* but only if you request one.

There are two main types of job pension scheme:

● *Final salary* means the pension you get is based on what you *earn* shortly before you retire.

● *Money purchase* means that the pension you get is based on the amount you and your employer *contribute* to your pension fund over the years and the investment growth of the assets (stocks, shares and interest on money on deposit) which this money is invested in.

With either type of pension you are allowed to contribute up to 15% of your earnings each year and your employer may contribute as much as he likes. But there are restrictions on the maximum pension you can get which are explained later in this Chapter. There are also limits on the amount of *surplus* the pension fund can accumulate, that is the amount of money in the pension fund which is more than the amount which it is estimated will be required to eventually pay the pensions.

Final salary job pension

Although this pension is called final 'salary', wage earners can also belong. It is called 'salary' because when pension schemes started they were only available to higher paid white collar workers. Nowadays most large companies extend the pension scheme to all groups of workers.

A final salary job pension normally depends on how long you have belonged to the pension scheme and what you are paid shortly before you retire (or leave the service of the employer), that is your *final salary*. There are some other restrictions laid down by the Inland Revenue which don't affect most employees. These are discussed at the end of this Chapter and given in detail in **Chapter 10 If you own your own company**. If your pay has fallen in the last few years your final salary can be higher than the actual salary in the last year provided the rules of your job pension allow this.

The most common way of calculating a final salary pension is to use a formula which can give you a pension of up to two-thirds of your final salary. Usually you get 1/60th of your final salary for each year you have belonged to the pension scheme.

For instance if you have been in the pension scheme for 20 years, you get 20/60ths (33%) of your final salary. If you have been in it for 30 years you get 30/60ths (50% or half) and so on. If you have been in the scheme for 40 years or more you get 40/60ths (66% or two-thirds) of your final salary. Two-thirds of final salary is the maximum pension you are allowed to get from a job pension scheme. The pensions people call this rate at which your pension accumulates the *accrual rate*.

Some schemes use 80ths instead of 60ths which means the best pension you can get *accrues* more slowly. For example after 20 years you get 20/80ths (25%) instead of 33% if your pension is accruing at 1/60th a year. After 30 years you get 30/80ths (38%) instead of 50% if your pension is accruing at 1/60th a year. The maximum pension you can get is still two thirds (53/80ths) but you would have to work for 53 years to get it (ie from 16 to 69). A normal 40 years in such a pension scheme would give a pension of 40/80ths (50%) instead of 40/60ths (66%).

The Civil Service pension and many other public sector pension schemes are different as they accrue at 80ths but pay a lump sum in addition to the pension. With most job pension schemes in the private sector you have a choice and your lump sum comes at the expense of accepting a lower pension. Lump sums are explained in **Chapter 3 How pensions work**.

There are a few pension schemes which accrue benefits faster, that is at fractions lower than 60ths, but these are rather rare. Such job pension schemes are very attractive to people who make a job move to a company with such a scheme when they are older, say, over age 40. However these schemes are still subject to Inland Revenue rules which restrict the overall amount of a job pension to a maximum of two-thirds of your final salary. So they do not necessarily give extra benefits to long serving employees.

Provided you are reasonably confident that you will stay with your present employer until you retire, a final salary job pension accumulating with 60ths or less or a public sector pension at 80ths with a lump sum in addition are the best types of pension to have.

That is because with a final salary pension, your pension is based on your salary on or near retirement and depends only on the number of years you have been working for your employer in that scheme. You can therefore plan your retirement income without worrying about how the stockmarket is performing or whether the pensions company's investment managers are taking the right decisions on your behalf. Final salary pensions are organised so that there is generally enough money available in the pension fund if the investment perform- ance does not come up to expectation. If the performance is not adequate, then the employer usually makes up any shortfall. It is virtually unheard of for a final salary pension scheme not to pay the pension which is due. But theoretically a final salary pension fund which does not have enough money to pay the pensions might only be able to pay a proportion of the pension due. This might happen because the company which set it up goes bust owing contributions to the fund.

One snag can occur for people who earn *overtime* or *bonuses* in that the overtime and bonus in some schemes does not count as part of your salary for pension purposes.

The advantage is that you don't pay contributions based on your overtime or bonus but when you retire your final salary does not include overtime and bonus earnings so you get a lower pension.

A number of job pension schemes also define your *pensionable earnings*, that is your earnings for the purpose of making contributions and working out your final salary, as your actual salary less the level of the State lower earnings limit for national insurance contributions. This reduces your contributions. When the job pension starts to be paid the amount of the basic State pension is deducted which can also reduce your pension.

For example if you are earning £10,000 a year and have earned yourself a pension of 40/60ths then you do not get 40/60ths of £10,000 which is £6,667. Instead you subtract £2,140 (the current annual rate of the State basic pension) from £10,000 and 40/60ths of the answer is £5,240.

Nevertheless if you are in a final salary pension scheme, particularly if you expect to stay with your present employer until you retire and probably even if you don't, you should probably remain in your job pension.

Money purchase job pension

A money purchase job pension works rather like a personal pension. The contributions are earmarked for an individual pension fund from which your benefits will be calculated. The pension fund is invested and managed by professionals and grows in value over the years. When you retire the fund is used to buy a *pension annuity* from a life insurance company which pays you a pension for the rest of your life.

Contracted-out or in?

The next point to check is whether your job pension is

contracted-out of the State earnings related (additional) pension ie if you are already not paying full national insurance towards the State earnings related (additional) pension. You should be able to find out whether your job pension is contracted-out or not by looking at the pension booklet provided by your employer. If the booklet does not say, or you don't understand it, then you should ask the person in your organisation responsible for pensions.

Alternatively look at your pay slip and try and work out what percentage of your pay has been deducted in national insurance contributions and relate it to the table of national insurance contributions in Chapter 4. If you are paying at the contracted-out rate, then your pension scheme is almost certainly contracted-out (the only other explanation which is not very likely is that your employer is deducting the wrong amount of national insurance).

Incidentally if your pension scheme was *contracted-out* before 6 April 1988, then it will be one based on your salary as before that date money purchase pensions were not allowed to be contracted-out.

A job pension scheme may allow employees who wish to remain in the State earnings related (additional) pension to do so while other employees who wish to opt out can also do what they want. If your job pension is contracted-in and you want to contract-out, you are allowed to take a special *minimum contribution personal pension* in order to do this. Or you can leave the job scheme and take out a personal pension.

When you belong to a contracted-out job pension both you and your employer pay national insurance contributions at a lower contracted-out rate on some of your earnings. In practice the difference is invested in your pension.

With a contracted-out personal pension you and your employer pay contracted-in contributions and the DHSS pays the difference between the contracted-in and con-

tracted out rates to your pensions company at least three
months after the end of the tax year in which you make
the contributions.

So with a job pension some of your money is invested
much more speedily.

Where an employer decides to start a new contracted-
out job pension scheme, or make an existing scheme into a
contracted-out one, the extra 2% *incentive* of part of your
earnings will be paid into your pension fund for up to six
years just like with a personal pension (five years if it is a
final salary job pension). This incentive is explained in
more detail in **Chapter 5 If you are an employee
without a pension.**

**But if you already belong to a contracted-out job
pension for two years or more and decide to leave
the pension (but not the firm) for a contracted-out
personal pension you do not get the 2% incentive
payment paid to your personal pension fund.**

Non-contributory

A non-contributory pension is one where you don't make
any contributions yourself – only your employer pays into
the scheme. As the pension is free, it is obviously a good
deal and you should almost certainly not contemplate
leaving it. Nevertheless it is worth finding out what you
are likely to receive from it.

Non-contributory schemes can be based on your final
salary or be money purchase. Either way if you are older
but have not been employed for many years with your
present employer, it could be worth your while topping up
with *additional voluntary contributions* of your own. This
is explained in **Chapter 7 Additional voluntary contributions to a job pension**.

If you belong to a non-contributory pension scheme and
you move jobs you usually can have a *transfer value* to

another job pension or to your own personal pension even though you have not paid any contributions yourself. There is more on this in **Chapter 13 Changing jobs**.

Retirement age

The normal retirement age from a job pension is no earlier than age 60 for men, 55 for women although there are some special exceptions to these rules. If you want to retire earlier you can do so up to ten years earlier than the normal pension age of the scheme, so the overall minimum age is 50 for a man and 45 for a woman. If you retire early there is usually a deduction from the pension you get because the pension is starting earlier than envisaged and will therefore have to be paid for longer. If you retire through ill health there is no minimum retirement age.

For instance say you are earning £10,000 a year and have been in a job pension scheme for 20 years. With a final salary pension at the normal retirement age of 65 you might get a pension of 20/60ths or £3,333 a year. But if you want to retire at 60 instead of the normal age of 65, you will be offered a lower pension, reduced by say 30%. So your pension would only be £2,333 a year. Some companies reduce the pension by much more, say 50% if you retire five years early. The reduction depends on how many years you retire early but varies between pension schemes. If you retire early as part of a compulsory early retirement scheme your pension may not be reduced by so much if your employer pays extra money into the pension scheme.

Generous treatment on early retirement, especially if you work for a large company, is a strong reason in favour of job pensions as opposed to personal pensions.

Money purchase job pensions theoretically should not make these deductions if you retire early. But you get a lower pension than you would at your normal retirement date because fewer contributions will have been paid and you will lose interest and growth on the investments in your pension fund for the period which you have decided to retire early. Also the younger the age you retire at, the lower the pension annuity.

Some life insurance companies deduct an extra charge from your pension fund which reduces the pension you get from a money purchase job pension if you want to retire early. This same sort of charge can apply to a personal pension but with a personal pension you can choose at the outset to have the earliest possible retirement date whereas with a money purchase job pension your employer decides on the normal retirement date.

Rising pension after retirement

One of the problems of retirement which is often overlooked is what happens to your pension after retirement. Getting a good pension is all very well, but if it is fixed and you live a long time, you can see your standard of living fall sharply during your retirement because of inflation.

Happily inflation is low at the moment – averaging between 3.5% and 5% a year. It has been much higher. But a job pension which is linked to the retail prices index, or pays increases from time to time which keep pace with inflation or average earnings increases, after pensions have started to be paid is much more valuable than one which does not.

If you retire on a pension of £6,667 a year, after 10 years that pension would need to rise to £9,404 to have the same purchasing power if inflation is 3.5% a year. After 20 years with inflation averaging 5% a year it would have to rise to £17,690. You can use the tables in **Appendix 1 How money grows: lump sum investments** or **Appendix 3 How inflation reduces the value of your money** to see the effect on your pension.

Appendix 1 will tell you for each £1,000 of your pension how much it needs to grow by to keep pace with inflation at the different rates given. And Appendix 3 shows you for each £1,000 of your pension, how much it is worth in today's money at various inflation rates.

If your job pension gives pension rises which meet all or part of the increase in the cost of living, then it is much more valuable than if the pension remains fixed. To replace such a job pension by taking out your own personal pension is very costly indeed. To save towards a personal pension which rises in line with the retail prices index will cost you around 70% to 80% more than contributions to one where the pension is fixed. To save towards a personal pension where the pension increases by 4% a year will cost you around 30% more than saving for a pension which is fixed.

How long is it paid?

Normally a pension is paid from your retirement date until you die. But if you drop dead a week after you retire and your pension stopped then, that would be a bit unfair on your wife or husband. Pensions can be *guaranteed* for a fixed period, say five or ten years. That means the pension continues to be paid at the full rate, plus any increases if it applies in your case, for normally five years (sometimes ten years) from your retirement date even if you die within that period. The money goes to your estate so who gets it depends on who you leave your money to.

Alternatively, but usually in addition, there may be provision for a pension for your widow, widower or dependants (a common law wife or husband whom you support or children under age 18 or in full time education). The pension is often half the pension which you were getting although it can be up to two-thirds of the maximum pension you are entitled to under the Inland

Revenue rules (which may be more than the actual pension you receive). There is no inheritance tax payable on these pensions.

Fringe benefits

Job pensions often don't just give you a pension at retirement. They also give you valuable life insurance and sick pay benefits. If you choose to opt out of a job pension scheme, you should also count the cost of replacing these benefits if your pension scheme offers them.

Life insurance

The advantage of life insurance with your job is that the life insurance cover is generally linked to your earnings and rises as your earnings rise. You also don't have to bother to take out the policy yourself or possibly undergo a medical examination by a doctor appointed by the life insurance company if you are not in tip-top health or want a large amount of cover.

The insurance cover given with your job does not have to be linked to the pension scheme but it generally is. It is normally some multiple of your *pensionable earnings*, say twice although the maximum allowed is four times. So if your pensionable earnings are £10,000 a year, your estate, or a named beneficiary you choose, or a *discretionary trust* with beneficiaries nominated by you, might get £20,000 – or £40,000 if your job pension pays the maximum amount.

You can get life insurance as part of a personal pension but the contributions you make are part of the total you can pay – so extra life insurance will mean a lower pension. See **Chapter 14 Life insurance with tax relief** for more details of this.

If you die before retirement

Most job pensions pay pensions to your widow, widower, or dependant (a common law wife or husband whom you support or children under 18) if you die while you are still working. The pension starts when you die. Your dependants don't have to wait until your retirement age. This is usually in addition to life insurance but may be instead of it.

The pension your widow or dependant get can be worked out in three main ways:

● The widows pension can be a fraction, say one third or 20%, of your salary when you die.

● The widows pension can be based on the number of years you could have belonged to the job pension scheme if you had lived until retirement. For instance if your pension scheme is based on 60ths of your final salary, you have been with the company for 10 years and you are 30 years away from retirement when you die, then your widow could receive a pension of half of 40/60ths of your current salary which is 20/60ths. So she gets a pension of 33% of your current salary.

● The widows pension is based on the number of years you have belonged to the pension scheme – in which case your widow would get a pension of half of 10/60ths of your current salary which is 5/60ths. So she gets a pension of 8.3% of your current salary.

Where the job pension is money purchase:

● The pension can depend on the value of the fund at the time of your death and generally speaking your widow or dependant is entitled to the value of the fund when you die or a pension based on it.

● Or it can be a fraction of your salary on death.

With a personal pension you can only get a widow's, widower's or dependant's pension as part of a special life insurance policy which is described in **Chapter 14 Life**

insurance with tax relief. Not all life insurance companies offer such policies which pay a pension, sometimes called *family income benefit*, through a personal pension policy. You can get a *family income benefit* policy without any limits on contributions from a life insurance company but you do not get tax relief on the premiums.

Ill or in an accidant

There is a *State statutory sick pay scheme* which pays sickness benefit through your pay cheque for up to 28 weeks. The rate for 1988–89 is £49.20 a week if you earn over £79.50 a week and £34.25 a week if you earn between £41 a week and £79.50 a week. Your employer may well pay you your full salary instead of these rates, or your full salary for part of the time.

However if you have been seriously ill, or been in a bad accident, most employers will want to give you notice if there is no prospect of you getting better for a very long time. Some job pension schemes pay a disability pension in these cases. How much the disability pension is worth depends on the rules of the pension scheme. The way it is worked out is likely to be the same as the way in which a pension for a widow or dependants is worked out. So it can either be quite worthwhile if it is based on the number of years you could have belonged to the pension scheme – or not very worthwhile if it depends on the number of years in which you have actually belonged to the pension scheme and you have not been in the scheme long. This depends on the rules of your employer's particular scheme.

Another way in which employers pay a disability pension is through *permanent health* or *sick pay insurance* where the employer pays the cost. This works along the same lines as the schemes you can get for yourself and which are described in the next paragraph.

You can get a disability pension of your own by taking out a *permanent health* or *sick pay insurance* policy from a life insurance company. This permanent health insurance pays a regular income, either fixed or increasing, to a chosen retirement date (or until you recover or die) after one, three, six, 12 or 24 months of disability. The longer the period of delay, and the earlier the policy stops, the cheaper the cost. An increasing income costs more than a fixed one. You can't get one of these policies if you are already in poor health when you start it. To pay £10,000 a year in sick pay (not increasing) starting after six months of sickness would cost you about £12 a month with a policy which you start when you are age 35, £16 a month if you start it at age 40, £18 a month at age 45, £24 a month at age 50. There is no tax relief on these premiums.

When you should leave

Broadly speaking you should leave a job pension scheme if it isn't very good for you. Come back to this section when you have got hold of the explanatory booklet of your job pension scheme. Here in summary are the determining factors of why you might be better off leaving a job pension:

● The shorter time you have been in your job pension, the less you have to lose by leaving it.

● The younger you are now, the less you have to lose by leaving a job pension scheme. Generally speaking if you are under about 30 to 35 and you change jobs, you won't get any benefit from contributions paid by your employer. So if you are this age or younger and don't think you will stay with your employer for very long, then don't stay in the job pension on account of the fact that your employer is making contributions; he may be but you are unlikely to see much if any of them. There may be other reasons for staying though.

● If you think you will change jobs shortly, you will be leaving your job pension scheme anyway. So leaving now won't make much difference.

● A money purchase job pension is similar to a personal pension which is also money purchase. You may not think your employer has chosen the best pensions company and may prefer to make your own choice. You could well lose the benefit of employer's contributions, but if you are young and move jobs that may be no loss. With a personal pension you have much more control over what happens to the money invested for your pension.

● Even if you belong to a final salary pension scheme, you may be better off leaving it. Schemes which you should consider leaving are those in the private sector where the pension benefits are worked out on 80ths of your salary (and there is no lump sum in addition) unless they pay pension increases after retirement.

● If you really don't care about pensions and just want to have higher take-home pay you can leave your job pension and not do anything instead. But be careful if your job pension is already contracted-out and you are on low earnings. You may find what you save in lower contributions to the job pension is equalled or almost equalled by higher national insurance contributions. This is most likely with a job pension scheme which asks you to make contributions only on your earnings above the lower earnings limit for the State pension (currently £41 a week). If you are young you would therefore be foolish not to opt out of the State earnings related (additional) pension and into a personal pension at the same time.

When you should stay

The reasons why you should not leave a job pension are more often than not the reverse of the reasons why you should leave:

● Job pension schemes work best if you stay in the same job, or rather stay with the same employer for at least two years. If you don't think you will leave your employer before retirement and the pension seems reasonable then you are unlikely to do better yourself through a personal pension. If you want a bigger pension you can always make *additional voluntary contributions*.

● Job pension schemes offered by very large organisations often, though not always, tend to offer better pensions and pensions which rise after retirement. If you work for a large employer like the Civil Service, you can change jobs within the Civil Service and still stay in the same pension scheme. If you work for a large company with many outlets around the country like a bank or building society or a department store, you can move locations, change jobs but stay with the same company and the same pension scheme. You should not normally leave such a pension scheme as the benefits are likely to be reasonably good – you may regret it later.

● The longer you have already been in a job pension scheme, the more worthwhile it is for you to stay in it because by leaving it you may reduce the amount of pension your previous membership of the scheme has earned you.

● The older you are, and the nearer to retirement age, the less keen you should be to opt out of your job pension scheme.

● You cannot set up a final salary personal pension. It is unlikely that a money purchase personal pension will be able to secure you a pension equal to the one you would have got from a final salary job pension. Don't leave just because you like the idea of having control of your own investments in your own personal pension fund.

Inland Revenue limits on a job pension

The only limit on your own contributions to a job pension is 15% of your earnings from the job – your employer can pay in as much as he likes. But there are limits on the maximum pension which you can receive from a job pension. Full details of the Inland Revenue limits are given in **Chapter 10 If you own your own company**. These limits depend on your *final salary* both when the job pension is a final salary scheme *and* in most cases when it is a money purchase scheme. The limits also depend on the number of years you have worked for the employer – which can be longer than the number of years which you have actually been in the pension scheme for.

It is possible that if your employer makes too high contributions to a money purchase pension – or the investments in which the pension fund is invested grow at an amazingly good rate, there may be a restriction on the pension you can draw which is related to your *final salary*. Unfortunately that is a problem that the average employee never has to worry about. However it can occur in the case of a company director setting up a special *director's job pension* for himself.

7
Additional voluntary contributions to a job pension

In theory a good job pension scheme can give you a pension of two-thirds your earnings after you have been in the scheme for 40 years. Relatively few people are in this position – and even fewer belong to a pension scheme which has been gathering such good benefits for the whole of the past 40 years.

Someone who receives a pension of two thirds their final salary is likely to have a higher income in retirement than when they were working. They will receive the State pension as well as the job pension assuming they retire at the State pension age or after. They will not have to pay national insurance contributions on their pension which they had to pay on their earnings. And they will have lower expenses as there are no longer the costs of travelling to and from work and possibly eating out at lunch time.

Over the years job pension schemes change – and often improve. But the improvement normally only applies for contributions made after the date of the change in the pension scheme rules. So although in theory you might earn a pension of two thirds your salary earnings plus the State pension, in practice you often will not.

If there have been alterations to the pension scheme you belong to since you started work with your current employer, you should check on what basis the previous benefits are worked out.

Also check whether your job pension is paid as an amount over and above the State basic pension at the time you retire. If that is the case your job pension may not be as high as the maximum it could be. If it is paid over and above the State basic pension, then on earnings of £10,000 a year your 'two-thirds' pension is two thirds of £10,000 less the basic State pension of £2,140 which is £5,240. But under the Inland Revenue rules your pension could be £6,667 and you could make up the difference with additional voluntary contributions.

The earlier contributions may not always result in you receiving a lower pension from them. In a few cases pension scheme changes made in 1978 mean you get a *higher* pension on contributions made before that date. That is because in 1978 a few large company pension schemes changed the basis of their schemes so that benefits are paid only above the State basic pension.

If you know your pension scheme rules have been changed since you joined you should ask the responsible person how your pension is worked out – and if possible get an estimate of the pension you are likely to receive.

You may not be counting on getting a large pension from your job scheme because you have not been with the firm long enough. If you join a company at age 45, unless you negotiate a special arrangement when you join, the best you can expect to get is a pension of 20/60ths from the scheme. If you have transferred some contributions from a previous job pension with another company you may of course get more than this. And if you have left a *preserved pension* with a previous job you can get a pension from that too.

You can use additional voluntary contributions to earn benefits for dependants and for pension increases from your job pension.

How to earn extra pension

To boost a pension from your job you can save using *additional voluntary contributions* or *AVC* and get full tax relief. The most you can contribute in additional voluntary contributions is 15% of your earnings in each tax year. But that 15% includes any contributions you make to your main job pension scheme.

For example if you earn £10,000 a year, then 15% of your earnings is £1,500. If your main job pension bases contribution on the whole of your earnings at say 5%, then you pay £500 to the main job scheme and are allowed to pay the rest, £1,000 in this case, as additional voluntary contributions less tax relief.

Now suppose your main job pension scheme is one where your contributions are on that part of your earnings above the lower earnings limit for national insurance contributions. Your earnings are £10,000. The lower earnings limit is £2,132 (for 1988–89). So your main job pension contribution is based on £10,000 minus £2,132 which is £7,868. And 5% of that figure is £393. You are allowed to pay up to £1,500 in pension contributions. So £1,500 minus £393 is £1,107 which you are allowed to pay as additional voluntary contributions.

But that's not the end of it. Suppose part of your earnings, say £1,000, comes from overtime or bonuses which the main job pension does not count as *pensionable earnings* although the Inland Revenue does.

Then your main job pension scheme contributions are based on £10,000 minus £1,000 which is £9,000, and possibly less the lower earnings limit of £2,132 which makes £6,868. Five per cent of £6,868 is £343. So in this case your additional voluntary contribution can be £1,500 minus £343 which is £1,157 – which is over three times as great as your ordinary contributions.

If you belong to a *non-contributory job pension* you are

entitled to make contributions up to the full 15% of your earnings. On £10,000 a year you can pay £1,500 a year in additional voluntary contributions less tax relief.

Extra lump sum?

If you start to make additional voluntary contributions on or after 8 April 1987 you have to take the whole of the amount you accumulate as a pension. There is no option to take part as a tax free lump sum as there is for the main job pension or for a personal pension. However additional voluntary contributions may still enable you to have a larger lump sum at retirement. The maximum lump sum allowed from the main job pension is based on your salary and period of service, not the actual amount of pension you receive.

If you started paying additional voluntary contributions before 8 April 1987 when you retire you can take part of the proceeds of these additional voluntary contributions as a lump sum. It appears that you can also raise your additional voluntary contributions within the 15% limit and possibly you can change the additional voluntary contributions scheme you are using. If you moved jobs on or after 8 April 1987 and want to pay additional voluntary contributions to a new pension scheme the 'no lump sum' rules will apply to you in the new scheme even if you were not liable to them in the old job pension scheme because you were in it before 8 April 1987.

Ordinary additional voluntary contributions

There are two types of additional voluntary contributions. With the ordinary version your employer offers the scheme. If you join your employer's additional voluntary contributions scheme the amount you have agreed to pay is deducted from your pay packet each month – along with your main job pension contributions if you belong to a contributory scheme. It can either be an agreed % of your earnings – say 5%, or a fixed monthly amount, say £50 with a chance to review the figure each year. You get tax relief through PAYE automatically.

Your employer can offer more than one additional voluntary contributions pension. So you may have a choice of a guaranteed scheme (which pays a fixed rate of return) run through the trustees of the job pension fund itself, or a scheme offered by a building society which pays interest on your money, or one offered by a life insurance company which offers a choice of different investments. The choice of investments is similar to the choice you can have with any money purchase job or personal pension and is described in **Chapter 8 How your money grows**.

You can join more than one additional voluntary contributions scheme if your employer offers that option and you no longer have to commit yourself to keep paying into the scheme for at least five years. There may be penalties with a life insurance company run scheme if you stop before you retire.

If you move jobs you can transfer your fund to another pension scheme but only together with the main scheme transfer value. There may be charges deducted from the fund when you do, especially if you transfer to a pension scheme which is not run by the same pensions company as the scheme you were paying to in the old job.

Free standing additional voluntary contributions

These work in a similar way to ordinary additional voluntary contributions except that instead of having the

contributions deducted from your pay cheque you pay
them direct to the pensions company as you would pay
contributions to a personal pension.

The contributions you pay have tax relief allowed at the
basic rate. If you are a higher rate taxpayer you have to
arrange to get the rest of your tax relief allowed in your
PAYE Notice of Coding or in a tax assessment later.

With free standing additional voluntary contributions
you are only allowed to have one at a time in any one tax
year. If you pay contributions monthly, that can be rather
inconvenient as you will have to remember to make the
change over in April when the tax year starts. Beware of
swopping companies with free standing additional voluntary contributions, because, as with life insurance company schemes there will often be a penalty charge
deducted from your pension fund when you do.

The minimum contribution depends on the pensions
company you choose. It is likely to be around £20 a month
or £200 a year and you can make single payments into the
scheme too with a minimum of £500 or possibly less with
some companies.

You can pay free standing additional voluntary contributions in addition to ordinary additional voluntary
contributions.

Contracting-out

If your job pension scheme is contracted-in to the State
earnings related (additional) pension scheme, instead of
paying extra voluntary contributions yourself, you can
divert part of your own and your employer's national
insurance contributions into a pension of your own.

To do this you have to *contract-out* of the *State earnings
related (additional) pension*. You get an extra payment of
2% of part of your earnings, called the *incentive*, for
several years too. Of course if your job pension scheme is

already contracted-out of the State earnings related
(additional) pension you can't do this.

You can contract-out of the State earnings related
(additional) pension in this situation by taking a special
minimum contribution personal pension or by using a *free
standing additional voluntary contributions* scheme. It is
better to use the personal pension as you get more tax
relief on your contributions that way.

The decision on whether to contract-out of the State
earnings related (additional) pension into a personal
pension is similar to that of an employee who does not
belong to a job pension and is considering whether to
contract-out of the State earnings related (additional)
pension into a minimum contribution personal pension.
This is covered in detail in **Chapter 5 If you are an
employee without a pension**.

Poor pension scheme

If your job pension scheme is rather poor, you would
probably be better to leave it for a personal pension rather
than trying to improve it with free standing additional
voluntary contributions. But you must not underestimate
the contribution which an employer's contributions can
make to your eventual pension.

It is not easy to assess whether you will be jumping out
of the frying pan into the fire. A pensions adviser cannot
be unbiased in giving you advice if he is paid by
commission as it will be much greater if he persuades you
to leave the main job scheme and take out a personal
pension rather than paying the (smaller) contributions to
a minimum contribution personal pension or free standing additional voluntary contributions scheme. Under the
Financial Services Act rules however, the adviser should
ignore the difference in commission and give you the
advice which is best for you.

8
How your money grows

How much your pension will be worth depends on how much money you, and your employer if you are in a job pension, put into your pension fund and how much the money grows. Your pension can be linked to many different types of investment and these have varying degrees of risk. Your money in the pension may grow steadily, very fast or may even fall in value. This Chapter explains the different types of investment and the risks and rewards involved.

Money purchase

The pensions referred to in this Chapter are *money purchase* pensions. These pensions are based directly on the performance of the investments bought with the money contributed to the pension fund up to the date of retirement. The other type of pension called *final salary* only applies to some job pensions. A final salary pension does not depend directly on investment performance but on the number of years you have belonged to it. All money purchase pension schemes have the same basic structure whether they are personal pensions, retirement annuities, job pensions or additional voluntary contributions.

Your contributions after deduction of any charges by the pensions company are invested in your own pension fund which is invested in a particular type of investment. These can be deposit schemes, guaranteed (sometimes known as non-profit), with-profits or investment linked. On retirement the accumulated pension fund is used to buy a *pension annuity* from a life insurance company which pays you a pension for the rest of your life. The higher your accumulated pension fund, the higher the pension you get when you retire. The aim is to choose the fund which will give you the maximum return with the minimum amount of risk you are prepared to take.

The descriptions in this Chapter are broadly speaking in order of risk from the least risky to the most risky.

Deposit based

With a deposit based pension fund you pay your contributions to a bank or building society which invests your money in your own pension fund where it gains interest. It is better than investing in a bank or building society account outside a pension because, like all pension funds, there is no tax on the interest. With banks or building societies which offer these types of pensions from 1 July 1988 there are published interest rates which are changed from time to time.

Deposit based pensions are also available from some unit trusts which make deposits in a number of different banks and building societies and swop around to get the best rate. These trusts should give a better return than deposits with one individual bank or building society but they may not because the trusts make higher charges than an individual bank or building society does.

There are also *cash funds, deposit funds* or *money funds* issued as an option with a *unit-linked* pension fund by life insurance companies. These work in the same way as the unit trust deposit funds and also should give a higher return than an individual bank or building society but may not because of heavier charges.

Deposit based pension funds are suitable for investing for a pension only in very narrow circumstances. These are:

● As an investment in a pension fund which is to be converted to a pension very shortly, that is within five years or less.

● For money awaiting the right time to reinvest in another form of investment. If you go for a deposit in a bank or a building society you must be sure that there is no penalty when you wish to switch to another type of investment with a different pensions company. Banks and building societies can act as agents for other types of pensions companies like life insurance companies or unit trusts, or own them as subsidiary companies, but they can only offer deposit based schemes themselves.

● If you are a very cautious individual and don't mind having a relatively low performance in return for complete peace of mind and the certainty that your investments will never fall in value. In that case you might also want to consider *guaranteed* or *non-profit* schemes.

Guaranteed or non-profit

These pension policies offer a fixed rate of return from the date of investment to the date when you have chosen to retire. When issued by a life insurance company, such policies often also offer a guaranteed pension. These are well worth considering if you are less than five years from your planned retirement date, especially so if you think interest rates are likely to fall between the date you start the pension plan and the date when you plan to retire.

With-profits

With-profits is one of the ways which life insurance companies distribute investment profits to people who invest in their pensions. It is a distinguishing feature of all with-profits pensions that once a bonus has been added to a pension fund, it cannot be taken away. However the rate at which the bonus is added in the future can vary from the current rate. There are a number of different ways in which with-profits pensions work. There are two main types:

Interest rate based

Interest rate based with-profits pensions, sometimes called *unitised with-profits*, are becoming increasingly popular. With these your money after deduction of the company's charges, is invested in a with-profits fund which is guaranteed to increase at a minimum interest or bonus rate which is usually 4% or 5% a year of the value of the fund. Each year a regular bonus rate is *declared* which should be well above the minimum, say, 8% a year. And each year the interest or bonus is added to your pension fund, either by raising the value of the fund or increasing the number of units you have. Once the bonus has been added it cannot be taken away.

When you want to retire there is usually another bonus added called a *final* or *terminal bonus*. This final bonus can double the amount of your pension fund.

Suppose you pay contributions of £1,000 a year (after any charges) for 25 years. With a bonus rate of 8% a year, on retirement your accumulated fund would grow to £78,954. The guaranteed rate of 4% a year would give a guaranteed accumulated fund of £43,312. A final bonus of 100% would double the value of the 8% a year accumulated fund to £157,908.

This accumulated fund is then used to buy a pension annuity, or part can usually be taken as a lump sum.

Endowment based

Endowment based with-profits policies work rather like endowment life insurance policies. They have a guaranteed *cash sum*, sometimes called a *sum insured* but it is only payable on retirement not if you die early. Sometimes this type of policy is called *pure endowment*. The guaranteed cash sum is about the same amount of money that your contributions would accumulate to if you got 4% interest on them. The guaranteed interest rate in the *interest rate based* with-profits pensions is a new way of expressing the *cash sum*.

With an endowment based type of pension a *reversionary bonus rate* which is a percentage of the cash sum is added to the cash sum each year. For example with premiums of £1,000 a year over 25 years the guaranteed cash sum might be £43,312. With a reversionary bonus rate of 2.43% a year the accumulated pension fund at retirement comes to the same £78,954 which with a final bonus of 100% comes to £157,908.

The reversionary bonus rate given in this example is a *compound* bonus rate which means that the bonus is worked out on the cash sum *plus* previously added bonuses. Some insurance companies quote a *simple* bonus rate which is based on the original cash sum only. A few have two simple rates of bonus – one on the original sum insured and one on the added bonuses. For a pension fund to grow from a guaranteed sum of £43,311 to £78,954 over 25 years using a simple bonus rate, the bonus rate is around 3.29% a year.

Because the cash sum is in terms of what you get when you retire, rather than the value of what you have paid in contributions, the actual *bonus rate* is lower for endowment type with-profits than for interest rate based with-profits. The fact that life insurance companies can give you the same benefits but show you a higher % bonus rate may account for the increasing popularity of the new interest rate bonus type of policy.

Regular versus final bonus

As far as the investor is concerned regular bonuses are better than a final bonus because once they are added to the pension fund they cannot be taken away. The final or terminal bonus is a large amount of money but depends very greatly on investment conditions shortly before the policy matures. The final bonus could, if necessary, be taken away altogether and your potential pension halved but you would have no right to complain. This has never happened but there is always a first time for everything.

Investment linking

The most common type of pension scheme offers the choice of a number of different kinds of investment funds within the same pension scheme. At the outset you choose which of the individual funds you want your contributions invested in. It can be more than one fund, subject to a minimum investment. Most companies offer a range of six to ten funds. A few offer a restricted choice of one or two. While others go completely over the top with a choice of hundreds of funds which you can link your pension fund to.

With most pensions companies you can switch your accumulated investment from one fund to another operated by the same pensions company. You fill in a form telling the pensions company your new choice. If you do this more than once a year there is usually a charge. So if you are invested in a fund of *equities*, that is shares in the

Stockmarket, and you don't think shares will be a good investment for a few years, you can switch all or part of your money to another fund which invests in property or fixed interest stocks.

You can even switch to another pensions company, but with a personal pension or retirement annuity you may be subject to extra charges.

Investment funds

There are basically ten types of investment funds to which a pension scheme can be linked:
- Cash deposit or money funds
- Index-linked government stock funds
- Currency funds invested in bank deposits
- Fixed interest funds (£ sterling)
- Property funds
- Fixed interest funds (foreign)
- Mixed or managed funds
- Equity funds
- International funds
- Broker funds

These are listed in order of risk, the least risky coming first. Usually the least risky investment gives a lower return on your money than a higher risk investment which may leap up in value but this is by no means always the case and sometimes the high risk investment takes a plunge which makes you wish you had stuck with a safer investment. Some of these funds are in fact individual *unit trusts* which can be linked to the pension fund. As far as pension funds are concerned it makes no difference whether your pension fund is invested in shares through a unit trust or directly in shares. The only snag is where the pension fund is linked to one, or invested in a number of unit trusts which are owned by another company (ie not a subsidiary of the pensions company) in which case you will be paying higher charges. Since 1 July 1988 some unit trust companies offer pension funds directly, not via a life insurance company.

Although these funds are listed in order of risk, there may be an overlap especially between equity and international funds. For instance an equity fund specialising in a narrow field like smaller companies may be more risky than an international fund which may spread its investments over a number of large and reliable companies which happen to be based in a number of different countries.

Cash deposits or money funds

Cash deposit or money funds invest your contributions in bank or building society accounts in the UK where your money gains interest. As explained above you do not need to have an investment linked pension scheme if you only want to keep your money in this type of investment and never want to move it out, you can invest direct with a bank or building society.

The advantages of having an investment linked pension scheme invested in cash deposits and money funds are that you can move your money out into another form of investment and the company can switch your money from one bank or building society account to another in order to find the best interest rates. The disadvantage of investing in a investment linked pension scheme through a life company instead of a pension scheme direct is that you will generally have heavier charges.

Index-linked stock funds

These funds invest in British Government index-linked stock, sometimes called index-linked Gilts. As not many stocks of this type exist, the number of stocks in the fund is limited. If you have a large amount of money, say £50,000, you might consider asking a pensions company to open a special fund for you investing in one single index-linked stock which *matures*, ie the Government repays the stock together with index-linking, just before your retirement. The money might come from an initial contribution or be switched from another fund.

Currency cash funds

These currency funds usually invest in bank deposits in foreign currency such as:
- US dollars
- Japanese yen
- German deutsch marks
- Swiss francs
- Australian dollars
- French francs
- Dutch guilders
- Italian lira

Some currency funds may also invest in £ sterling. An investment worth considering if you think the £ will depreciate against these foreign currencies before you retire.

Fixed interest funds (£ sterling)

These funds invest in:
- British Government fixed interest stock known as gilts
- UK company loan stock
- UK company debenture stock
- UK preference shares
- Foreign government stock in £ sterling
- Eurosterling issues

They do not include British Government index-linked stock which is described above and is less risky.

When interest rates fall, the value of fixed interest stock rises. This is the time to sell to make a capital gain. When interest rates are high, the value of the stock is low and this is the time to buy provided you don't expect interest rates to go even higher. A good pension scheme manager will make good use of these fluctuations to make your investment grow in value by selling the fixed interest stock when it reaches a high value and reinvesting when interest rates rise and the value of the stock has fallen. The time to invest in these funds is when interest rates are high and are expected to fall. Remember this when you choose to invest in this type of fund.

Property funds

Property funds invest directly in property or property shares although the fund may contain money invested in bank deposits or fixed interest stock which is waiting to be invested in property. In some cases property funds have no holdings in property but solely invest in property company shares and cash.

Property funds may contain the following types of property and holdings:
● Offices
● Shops
● Factories
● Warehouses
● Residential property
● Property company shares
● Property development (eg building new shops and offices)
● Fixed interest stock
● Cash on deposit
● Non-property unit trusts or shares

Many property funds have not done well over the past ten years although recently with the Stock Market crash, they have done better. This is because many people preferred investing in equity (share) funds. Money in property funds was often tied up in office property which did not rise in value. Shop property has now become fashionable but it is difficult to predict how stable this sector is. If you want to invest in a property fund, consider it a long term investment and check through the portfolio of properties in a reference book or the managers' report to fundholders which they will send on request. Residential property and agricultural land can be highly speculative and depends very much on the location. It is therefore extremely risky.

Fixed interest funds (foreign)

These funds invest in fixed interest and Government stock in foreign currencies. They are riskier than UK fixed interest stock because the foreign currencies fluctuate against £ sterling and as they are invested in different countries, the pension scheme manager has more to look out for.

Not many exist but if you think the foreign currencies will rise in value against the £, they could be a worthwhile investment. To be on the safe side, choose a fund which is invested in major markets like Japan, West Germany and the United States.

Mixed or managed funds

These funds are called mixed funds, managed funds or occasionally balanced or 3 way funds. They contain a mixture of:
● Shares and/or unit trusts both in the UK and overseas
● Property either directly or in property development
● Fixed interest or Government stock
● Cash on deposit

The pensions company which runs your pension scheme hopes to choose the best of all these types of investments and switches from one to another when a profit is to be made. Sometimes there might be only shares or unit trusts in a mixed fund but a good spread will reduce the risk.

A good fund for people who don't want to choose the funds themselves but want a spread of investments.

Equity funds

Equity funds usually invest in:
● Ordinary shares in the UK
● Unit trusts which specialise in UK shares
They may also include:
● UK fixed interest and government stock
● UK index-linked government stock
● Overseas shares
● Unit trusts specialising in overseas shares

Equity funds, often called *stockmarket managed funds*, have done very well in the past few years until the Stock Market crash in October 1987. The prospects for equity funds over the next few years in my opinion are not good but if you save regularly month by month you will have money invested which will be able to gain from the recovery.

UK equities with a high yield Some equity funds specialise in shares providing a *high income yield* which means that the dividends paid by the shares are higher than normal. These shares are less likely to fall as strongly as other shares and are recommended.

UK general equities UK general equity funds can be more risky than those with a high yield as they are as likely to go down or up as high yielders but they do not have as high an income yield.

UK equities in one sector Some funds concentrate on one particular sector in the UK stock market eg smaller companies. These can be very risky – if you choose the right sector at the right time, your fund can make a lot of money but when the Stock Market is generally falling, this type of share tends to fall more and lose you a lot of money.

International funds

International funds invest in overseas shares although some funds include UK shares. Some international funds concentrate on a particular area eg Europe, North America, Far East or Australasia while other funds concentrate on a particular country eg United States, Japan or Germany. Other funds specialise further and concentrate on one particular sector of one country eg Japanese technology shares.

International funds investing in many countries These funds spread over a wide range of countries and invest in many different currencies and economies. If you feel that shares abroad will do better than shares in the UK, then you should consider this type of fund. It does, however, usually have a lower income return than UK shares. One way to spread your risk is to invest partly in an international fund and partly in a UK equity fund.

International funds in one area abroad If you choose the right area, your fund can grow considerably but there is quite a risk involved and you must follow what is going on in that area quite closely. Political stability is a major consideration in making any foreign investment because controls on foreign investment and/or poor economic controls can change an excellent investment into a dud very quickly.

International funds in one country Investing in one country overseas is even more risky than choosing a larger area. If you know the country well and can judge how well the currency and economy of the country are doing, you will lessen your risk. Countries in which a fund might invest include:
- Australia
- Belgium
- Canada
- France
- Germany
- Holland
- Hong Kong
- Japan
- Malaysia
- Scandinavia
- Singapore
- Spain
- Switzerland
- United States

International funds in one sector of one country These types of funds are normally highly speculative and not recommended in today's markets.

Broker managed fund

These funds are no more risky than other types of equity or international funds. The idea is that your own stockbroker, insurance broker or investment adviser makes an arrangement with a pensions company (usually a life insurance company). The broker is usually given a large choice of funds in which he can switch your pension fund investments into, consisting of the types of funds described above and also many individual unit trusts to which pension funds can be linked. The broker switches between these funds and the cash deposit fund and often manages the fund actively. You have to pay the broker extra charges and you hope he will do better than leaving your money with the pensions company in their managed or mixed pension fund which on the face of it should do just as well. No one can really say whether broker funds will do better than pensions company funds – some will do better and others will do worse.

How to choose

There sometimes seems to be too much choice. Which type of fund you should choose partly depends on how long you have to go to retirement:

● With over 15 years to retirement choose between funds invested in *mixed or managed linked, property linked, with-profits, currency funds, equity linked, international linked, index-linked stock.*

● With 4 to 15 years to go choose from between *property linked, with-profits, fixed interest funds (£ sterling), fixed interest funds (foreign), currency fund linked to bank deposits, cash deposit or money funds.*

● With less than 4 years use *cash deposit or money funds* or *non-profit.*

9
If you are self-employed

This Chapter is mainly for people who work for themselves either as a sole trader or a partner. If you own and work for your own company you should also read **Chapter 10 If you own your own company**

Not much State pension

Being self-employed, you don't belong to the State earnings related (additional) pension scheme so you don't have the problem of deciding whether to opt out of it or not. Of course if you have just started on your own or you used to be an employee or a company director since 1978, you will get some State earnings related (additional) pension when you retire. You can get an estimate of how much this is by asking for the leaflet *NP38 Your future pension* from a local office of the Department of Health and Social Security (DHSS) and completing and posting off the tear off form to the DHSS. Being self-employed though, you won't want to rely on the State for your pension and will be as interested as anyone in a personal pension.

Retirement annuities

You may well have recently taken out a new pension scheme before 1 July 1988. Up till that date individual pensions were called *retirement annuities* and the rules are slightly different. Now they are called *personal pensions*.

Retirement annuities are always issued by life insurance companies and are often called *policies*. You cannot start a new retirement annuity any more but you can continue paying contributions or *premiums* and you can often increase your contributions or make extra one-off contributions until you reach age 75.

If under the original rules of the retirement annuity policy you have taken out, the life insurance company allows you to pay increased contributions to the same retirement annuity (ie under the same policy number) you can raise the amount you pay within the overall limits (normally 17.5% of your earnings, more over age 50). This can be either as increased regular contributions or an extra lump sum. This is the case even if your original retirement annuity was for a lump sum only provided the rules allow you to make additional contributions under the same policy number.

So suppose you are paying contributions of £50 a month to a retirement annuity. If you want to raise these to £80 a month, or pay a single extra contribution of £1,000 then you can, provided the life insurance company's rules for the retirement annuity allow this.

Similarly if you made a one-off contribution of £1,000 originally, provided the retirement annuity allows it, you can now start making regular contributions of, say, £100 a month or additional lump sum payments of any amount.

The contribution limits for retirement annuities and personal pensions are combined. These are 17.5% of your earnings up to age 50 with higher limits from age 50 to 75.

The contribution rules are the same for retirement annuities as they are for personal pensions and are explained in **Chapter 3 How pensions work**. There is also the ability to make use of previous year's unused allowances and count contributions paid in one year as if they had been paid in the previous year.

Extra or less lump sum

If you can, should you raise your contributions to an existing retirement annuity instead of starting a new personal pension? Retirement annuities are better than personal pensions in one respect only. The cash lump sum available on retirement depends on a formula which can let you take a bigger part of the proceeds of your pension as a tax free lump sum than the fixed 25% of your

Table 9
Retirement annuity lump sum as a % of pension fund

Age when you start to draw pension	%
Man	
60	28.5
65	30.7
70	33.7
75	37.5
Woman	
60	26.3
65	28.0
70	30.4
75	33.7

accumulated fund which is available to a personal pension.

The formula means that you can get a lump sum of up to 37½% of your accumulated pension fund if you are a man who retires at age 75.

With a retirement annuity the lump sum is worked out as three times the *residual pension*; the residual pension is the pension which you get after having taken the lump sum. As the pension you get depends on your age and whether you are a man or a woman, the lump sum also depends on these factors.

The snag is that the lower the pension you get the lower the lump sum you are entitled to with a retirement annuity. So if you are a woman retirement annuities are not such a good deal as women get lower pensions than men of the same age. Some examples of possible lump sums as a percentage of the accumulated pension fund are shown in Table 9 opposite.

If your retirement annuity is with a life insurance company which offers poor value for money in the *pension annuity* rates it pays on your retirement annuity, then you will get a smaller lump sum. If you use the *open market option* to obtain your pension from another company, then the lump sum is always 25% of the accumulated fund as with a personal Pension.

Retirement annuity or personal pension

Apart from the possibility of a higher lump sum, personal pensions are better than retirement annuities giving more flexibility on retirement age.

Retirement age

With a retirement annuity retirement age is normally between ages 60 and 75. You can only retire earlier if you belong to certain professions, notably professional sports-people who can retire at 35 or you are in ill health. But if you belong to those categories you lose out as the lump sum you can get under a retirement annuity will generally be much less than the one you can get under a personal pension. With a personal pension retirement age is between ages 50 and 75.

Tax relief

Tax relief is given at the same rate to both retirement annuities and personal pensions. However although for employees with personal pensions basic rate tax relief is given by deduction from the contributions, for the self-employed the contribution must be paid in full. You get tax relief later in your tax assessment.

When to pay contributions

You may be someone who just cannot save unless you make a commitment to putting a regular amount away every month. If you are like that then that is what you should do. Save as much as you can afford.

But if you are someone who is capable of planning, you can use a single contribution to a personal pension or retirement annuity to keep your income tax bill as low as possible.

You pay tax as a self-employed person or as a partner on the profits of your business in your accounting year. You decide when the accounting year ends when you start your business (you can change it – though the actual date makes little difference when it comes to pension planning).

It takes time for your accountant to work out the actual level of your profits in any particular accounting year. You also have to relate these to your other income and any other tax allowances to determine what rate of tax you pay.

The contributions you make to a personal pension or a retirement annuity are subject to a maximum scale of 17.5% of your earnings for each tax year (more if you are over 50). The detailed scales are given in Table 1 in **Chapter 3 How pensions work**.

If you don't use up the allowance in one year, you can carry them forward for up to six tax years. You can also opt to treat contributions paid in the current tax year as having been paid in the previous year. These rules are also described in detail in Chapter 3.

You should aim to use up your pension allowances in years in which you pay tax at higher rates and avoid years when you are not a taxpayer.

If you are always a basic rate taxpayer remember that the basic rate of tax has been falling in most years recently. So if you make a pension contribution this tax year (1988–89) the basic rate of tax is 25% which is the rate you get tax relief at.

But if you have enough allowances available last year (or from previous years carried forward to last year) and you choose to have the contribution treated as having been paid last year (1987–88) you get tax relief at 27%.

In years when there is no reduction in the basic rate of tax there are no tax planning advantages for paying in one year rather than another so you should make your contributions when it is most convenient for you to do so. If the tax rates rise, then it is better not to have the contributions treated as having been paid last year.

The same considerations apply to higher rate taxpayers. In 1987–88 the higher rates of tax started at 40% and rose to 60%. In 1988–89 there is only one higher rate of tax which is 40%. Obviously if your top tax rate last tax year was more than 40%, it's worth getting contributions treated as being paid last year rather than this if you can.

The best time to decide when to make a lump sum contribution to a personal pension or retirement annuity is in March each year just after the Budget. You then have a choice of three tax years in which your contributions can be treated as paid.

You can either pay contributions before 6 April and have them allowed against tax in the current tax year, or the previous tax year if you choose. Or you can wait and pay them on or after 6 April and they will be set against your tax in the next tax year.

For example suppose you were in this position in March 1988. The basic rate of tax for 1987–88 was 27%; the rate for 1986–87 was 29% and the rate announced in the 1988 Budget for 1988–89 was 25%.

So with a contribution of £1,000 you had a choice of getting tax relief at 25% if you delayed paying until on or after 6 April 1988. Or you got tax relief at 27% if you paid before 6 April 1988. Or had you paid before 6 April 1988 and chosen, also before 6 April 1988, to have your contribution treated as if paid in the 1986–87 tax year, you could have had tax relief at 29%.

The difference between making the best and worst decision in this case where the contribution is £1,000 is 4% which is £40. If you paid 60% higher rate tax in one year and only 40% in the next, then the difference is 20% or £200.

10
If you own your
own company

The fact that your employer pays contributions to a job pension is no advantage if you are in effect both employer and employee as a director of a family company which you own and work for.

The question is whether you should set up a *director's job pension* (sometimes known as a *top hat pension* for yourself or save towards your pension through a *personal pension*. The decision depends on a great many variables and you need to get advice from a knowledgeable pensions broker or chartered accountant, or more likely both, before you commit yourself to a particular method.

Maximum contributions to a job pension

There are theoretically no limits on what a company can contribute to a *director's job pension*. However the Inland Revenue has the right to refuse tax relief for corporation tax on the company's contributions if it thinks the company is paying contributions which are higher than necessary to fund the pension based on your current earnings.

For example you won't be able to get the company to make overlarge contributions to the pension fund, say £10,000 a year, while year after year you remain on low earnings, say only £2,200 a year. However the contributions the company can make are much larger than the contributions you can make to a personal pension.

Inland Revenue limits on the maximum job pension

There are restrictions on the amount of pension you are allowed to receive from a job pension. These depend on Inland Revenue limits which are explained here. The maximum pension you are allowed to receive depends on the number of years you have worked for the firm:

● If you joined a job pension scheme on or after 17 March 1987 you can get the maximum pension provided you have worked for the firm for 20 years or more; you don't have to have been in the pension scheme for 20 years.

If by retirement age you have worked for the firm for less than 20 years, then the maximum pension you can receive is reduced pro rata. For example after 10 years the largest pension you can draw is half the pension you can get after 20 years or more.

● If you joined the pension scheme before 17 March 1987 you only have to have worked for the firm for 10 years to get the maximum pension.

If you already have a job pension scheme you may be better off making extra contributions to it rather than starting a new job pension scheme where you will be liable to the new rules which apply to job pension schemes started on or after 17 March 1987.

Secondly, although the actual pension you get from a money purchase scheme depends on the amount you and your company have made in contributions and how the

Table 10

Inland Revenue limits for maximum job pensions

Years of service	Maximum pension as a fraction of pension scheme if you joined:	
	before 17 March 1987	on or after 17 March 1987
1	1/60th	1/30th
2	1/30th	2/30ths
3	1/20th	1/10th
4	2/30ths	4/30ths
5	1/12th	1/6th
6	4/30ths	1/5th
7	8/30ths	7/30ths
8	2/5th	8/30ths
9	16/30ths	3/10ths
10	2/3rds	1/3rd
11	2/3rds	11/30ths
12	2/3rds	2/5ths
13	2/3rds	13/30ths
14	2/3rds	14/30ths
15	2/3rds	1/2
16	2/3rds	16/30ths
17	2/3rds	17/30ths
18	2/3rds	3/5ths
19	2/3rds	19/30ths
20 or more	2/3rds	2/3rds

value of your pension fund has performed, the limit your pension is in terms of your *final salary*.

For someone who owns and works for his or her own company, final salary is normally defined as the average of your earnings over the last three years before you retire. However if your earnings were higher in earlier years you can instead use the average of any three consecutive years ending not more than 10 years before retirement.

There is another definition of final salary which can be used instead but only applies if at the time you retire (and for the 10 previous years) you own or control less than 20% of the shares in your company and you are earning less than £100,000 a year. Final salary by that definition is the highest single year's earnings in the five years before retirement. These definitions apply if you join a job pension scheme on or after 17 March 1987. If you joined earlier the definitions are less restrictive.

Final salary can include basic salary or wages, bonuses, commission and benefits in kind but excludes any share option profits granted on or after 17 March 1987 which are taxed as income and any compensation for termination of employment.

Salaries used to calculate final or average salary can be raised by the retail prices index (apart from the last year) to give a current value.

Personal pensions

The alternative to keeping a job pension scheme going or setting up a new job pension is to take out a personal pension. As far as you are concerned the main difference between a *personal pension* and a *job pension* is the differences in the amount you are allowed to contribute and the amount you can draw as a pension when you retire.

In most other respects job pensions which you can set up for your own company on a money purchase basis are very similar to personal pensions, or retirement annuities which you may have taken out in the past. The question of whether you should set up a pension scheme for your employees is covered by **Chapter 11 If you employ people**. Obviously if you have a pension scheme for your employees, you might as well include yourself and your husband or wife assuming he or she also works for the company.

To save you turning back to Chapter 3, here is a summary of the amount you are allowed to pay in contributions to a personal pension. If you are 50 and under it is 17·5% of your earnings; 51 to 55 20%; 56 to 60 22·5%; 61 to 75 27·5%.

A job pension therefore has an advantage over a personal pension if you envisage paying contributions to a job pension scheme which exceed the maximum contributions for a personal pension. If you are in that position your profits from your company are likely to be over £30,000 a year.

Should you trade as a company?

The choice of which type of pension scheme you should take may concentrate your mind on whether your business is incorporated in the most efficient way for your circumstances. Tax changes over the past few years have considerably shifted the advantages away from small businesses trading as companies in favour of them trading as *partnerships* or as self-employed *sole traders*. If taxation was the only consideration you should always start a new small business as a self-employed sole trader or a partnership.

After you have read this Chapter you may consider that it would be better for your business to be run without a company and for you to convert it into a sole trader or partnership. The best person to give you advice on this is your accountant but you should also consult your bank manager and pension adviser if you have one.

If you have an existing job pension scheme through the company, the effect on this will also have to be considered (see later in this Chapter). If your existing pension arrangements are through a retirement annuity or a personal pension, then they are unaffected by whether you trade as a company or as a sole trader or partnership.

In favour of a company

1. Companies have limited liability so you may be able to avoid risking all your assets. But banks often require a personal guarantee on overdrafts. If you give one, and do not ask for it to be lifted once you are established, you are not benefiting from limited liability.

2. It is simpler to sell a business as a company as you just have to sell the shares. If you have an exchange of shares with a big company, you will be able to defer capital gains tax although business retirement relief at age 60 or over reduces this tax considerably.

3. There are no fixed contribution limits on how much you can contribute to a job pension scheme as an employer although you are not allowed to pay more than it is estimated you need to pay the maximum pension to the employees who belong to the scheme. The maximum pension paid as a pension when you retire is determined by Inland Revenue limits (described above) which depend on how long you have worked for the company rather than how long you have been in the pension scheme. It can therefore be easier to 'catch up' with a job pension rather than a personal pension as you can normally make larger contributions in the years before retirement with a job pension than with a personal pension.

4. You should set up a company, rather than a partnership, for any joint venture with someone else unless you are in a partnership with your wife or husband, or in a professional partnership like a firm of solicitors or chartered accountants. If you fall out with the partner, which frequently happens, the divorce is probably easier with a company.

Against a company

National insurance contributions are normally much higher if you run your business as a company. You can find yourself paying five times as much, possibly thousands of pounds more if your joint earnings are £30,000 a year or more with a husband and wife running their affairs as a company instead of a partnership. If the four points above in favour of a company don't apply, you are normally better off running your business as a sole trader or a partnership. This is best illustrated by some examples.

Self-employed Suppose your business makes £30,000 a year profits. You get a personal tax allowance for 1988–89 of £4,095 (married). The next £19,300 is taxed at 25% (£4,825) and the rest at 40% (£2,642). That comes to £7,467 in income tax.

There are also national insurance contributions totalling £770.54 (explained in **Chapter 4 The State pension**) consisting of £210.60 at Class 2 and £699.93 at Class 4. You are allowed tax relief on half your Class 4 contributions but no Class 2. Tax relief (in this case at 40%) on half of £699.93 comes to £139.99. So your total national insurance comes to £770.54. So your total deductions are national insurance £910.53 plus income tax £7,467 less tax relief £139.99 which is £8,238. So you take home £30,000 minus £8,238 is £21,762.

As a company with a salary Now consider you make the same £30,000 profit as a company before you pay yourself. You decide to pay all your profits out as director's salary. The company pays no tax because your director's salary counts as an expense.

As you pay employer's national insurance on your directors salary, the £30,000 must include your employer's national insurance. The rate is 10.45%. So if you pay yourself a salary of £27,162 plus employer's national insurance contributions of £2,838 that uses up your £30,000 profit.

If you know your profits and want to work out what amount after employer's national insurance would exactly use them up, then multiply the figure by 100 and divide by 110.45.

Your national insurance as an employee is 9% of £15,860 (the upper earnings limit) which is £1,427. So your total national insurance is £1,427 as an employee plus £2,838 as employer which comes to £4,265.

Your tax bill is worked out on the same way as if you are self-employed except that it is on an income of £27,162. You get a personal tax allowance for 1988–89 of £4,095 (married). The next £19,300 is taxed at 25% (£4,825) and the rest at 40% (£1,507). That comes to £6,332 in income tax. So £6,332 income tax plus £4,265 national insurance makes a total of £10,597. Subtract that from £30,000 profit and you have a take home pay of £19,403.

Take home pay compared By running your own business as a company your take home pay after tax and national insurance is £19,403 compared with £21,762 as a self-employed person. You are £2,362 a year better off as self-employed.

You can reduce the national insurance bill slightly by opting out of the State earnings related (additional) pension. You should only do this if you would get a larger pension by doing so as explained in **Chapter 5 If you are an employee without a pension**.

As a company with dividends You can avoid most of
the national insurance contributions by paying yourself a
low salary, say £2,200 which is just enough to qualify you
for the State basic (flat rate) pension. But there is a big
snag with this when it comes to pensions. If you follow this
example the maximum contribution you can make to a
personal pension is 17.5% of £2,200 which is £385 a year.
That won't earn you much pension. And in that situation
a *director's job pension* may be almost impossible to
accumulate. So you shouldn't bother with this idea.

National insurance for husband and wife

National insurance for employees (ie for you as a company
director) and for the self-employed, do not have to be paid
on earnings above a certain maximum limit (£15,860 in
1988–89). With a business which employs both husband
and wife there is a choice each year as to who gets what
share of the profits as income.

It is generally best giving one partner (or director) most
of the earnings and the other just enough to keep him or
her in the lowest 5% band of national insurance contributions (ie below £3,639 a year), or if they are self-employed,
enough to keep them below the level at which Class 4
national insurance contribution starts (£4,750 for 1988–
89).

For example take the example of a couple with profits
they can convert into earnings of £30,000. Depending on
the way they split the earnings between them and
whether they are company directors of self-employed,
they can pay quite different amounts of national insurance.

A husband or wife can also be an employee of the other
spouse who is self-employed but this has no advantage

other than in the first year of a new business in order to create a loss for tax accounting purposes. How this compares is shown in Table 11. The lowest national insurance is paid where there are two partners and one takes the lions share of the earnings.

A wife who is paying the *reduced rate* of national insurance does not pay any Class 2 contributions and pays Class 1 employee's national insurance at a lower rate. Class 4 and Class 1 employer's are unaffected – see **Chapter 4 The State pension**.

Employers' national insurance contributions are on a scale starting at (contracted-in rate) 5% for earnings from £2,132 a year to £3,639 a year; 7% on earnings from £3,640 to £5,459; 9% on earnings from £5,460 to £8,059 and 10.45% on earnings of £8,060 and over. The contributions are based on all your earnings at the highest rate. So if you have an employee who earns £3,000, the national insurance is 5% of £3,000; if he earns £10,000 it is 10.45% of £10,000. Full details in Table 12 on page 143.

Tax for husband and wife

Under present tax rules a wife's earnings count as part of her husband's income. The husband gets a *married allowance* (£4,095 in 1988–89) and the wife gets a wife's earnings allowance of £2,605 which are used to reduce the income before tax rates are applied. Otherwise their earnings are added together and if the earnings after deduction of these allowances plus other outgoings like mortgage interest and pension contributions come to more than the allowances then the 25% basic tax rate is applied. The 40% higher rate of tax applies on the excess over £19,300.

Going back to our example of a couple with earnings of £30,000 between them. Their personal tax allowances are £4,095 plus £2,605 which is £6,700. Suppose they pay

le 11

and national insurance for husband and wife in the same
iness

ings	£	Employees NI contributions			Income tax £	Total tax and NI £	Take home pay £
		Class 1 £	Class 2 £	Class 4 £			
␣er 1	25,250	Nil	211	560[1]	5,567	6,338	18,912
␣er 2	4,750	Nil	211	Nil	858	1,069	3,681
␣	30,000	Nil	422	560	6,425	7,407	22,593
␣er 1	27,270	Nil	211	560[1]	6,375	7,146	20,124
␣oyee 2	2,600	130	Nil	Nil	Nil	Nil	2,470
␣loyer's ␣ntrib.	130	Nil	Nil	Nil	Nil	130	-130
␣	30,000	130	211	560	6,375	7,276	22,464
␣er 1	15,000	Nil	211	565[2]	3,100[3]	3,876	11,124
␣er 2	15,000	Nil	211	565[2]	3,100	3,876	11,124
␣	30,000	Nil	422	1,130	6,200	7,752	22,248
␣ctor 1	23,702	1,427	Nil	Nil	5,132	6,559	17,143
␣loyee 2	3,639	182	Nil	Nil	416	598	3,041
␣loyer's ␣ntrib.	-2,659	Nil	Nil	Nil	Nil	2,659	-2,659
␣	30,000	1,609	Nil	Nil	5,548	9,816	17,525
␣ctor 1	13,581	1,222	Nil	Nil	2,546	3,768	9,813
␣ctor 2	13,581	1,222	Nil	Nil	2,744	3,966	9,615
␣loyer's ␣ntrib.	2,838	Nil	Nil	Nil	Nil	2,838	-2,838
␣	30,000	2,444	Nil	NI	5,488	10,770	16,590

␣es contracted-in to State earnings related pension. [1]After tax relief at 40% on half Class 4 ␣ɔ,ution. [2]After tax relief at 25% on half Class 4 contribution. [3]Assumes separate taxation of wife's ␣gs and no married allowance; from 1990 £372 less tax in this example.

£3,000 mortgage interest. That makes a total of £9,700 of their income which is untaxed. The first £19,300 is taxed at 25% which leaves the balance of £1,000 to be taxed at the 40% higher tax rate.

Assuming they make pension contributions of at least this amount they have no need to ask for *separate taxation of the wife's earnings* to cut their tax bill nor to equalise their earnings to benefit from this.

Indeed your joint earnings must normally be over around £40,000 (assuming you pay £5,000 worth of tax allowable mortgage interest and pension contributions) for it to be worthwhile to make this election.

From 6 April 1990 husbands and wives will be taxed completely separately in all cases. That will make no difference to the problem of national insurance contributions if you are both company directors or partners. Any levelling of income to benefit from more tax at the 25% basic rate is still offset by extra national insurance contributions which are paid when two people share an income from a business rather than one.

When a personal pension is the right choice

The lower your earnings and profits from your business, the less you feel you need or want to pay to a pension, the better off you are with a *personal pension* as opposed to a *job pension*. Nevertheless job pensions can be more complex to administer and need more consideration than personal pensions so I would suggest that anyone with profits under £20,000 a year from his or her company should probably save towards a pension using a personal pension rather than a job pension.

However someone with that level of profits should seriously consider converting to become a sole trader or a partnership. The figure is arbitary and is put in for general guidance only. If you think you are better off trading as a partnership rather than a company then consult your accountant.

National insurance contributions for employees and the self-employed stop at age 60 for women and 65 for men but employer's contributions continue whatever the age of the employee or company director.

When a job pension is better than a personal pension

If you have to stay as you are as company directors, then it is important to decide how much you pay into a job pension. You must decide how much you want and need to spend to live on – and how much you want to save towards a pension. The less you pay yourself as a salary, the less national insurance you pay. If you pay the difference between your profits and what you pay yourselves as director's fees into a job pension, you pay neither national insurance contributions as an employer or employee, nor corporation tax nor income tax on the money you have put into the pension. You would have to pay these contributions if you took it out as a salary and then put it in a personal pension.

But remember if you take a lower salary to escape national insurance, if you are in a job pension you have to stop doing this in the last three years before retirement otherwise you may jeopardise the maximum pension which can be paid out. And if you die before retirement there are further complications.

Who should have the pension

How much you contribute to a job pension depends on how

much you have to contribute. If you have followed the advice to pay Director 2 a small salary of £2,600 and the main earnings go to Director 1 you need not worry that Director 2 will be without a pension. On retirement the pension can be on a *joint life* basis which means that up to two thirds of it will be paid to the widow or widower of the pensioner until they die.

There could be a snag of course if you split up. The answer may be to alternate who has the higher earnings. For a few years Director 1 gets the higher earnings, then Director 2 does. So assuming earnings from the company do not fluctuate wildly, then on average each director will accumulate a pension fund of similar value.

Equalising pensions on retirement

While you are working it is better not to equalise your earnings so that you don't pay too much in national insurance contributions. Once you have retired, the reverse is true and you are best off having equal incomes and pensions after retirement when national insurance contributions are not payable.

That is because you can benefit from the separate taxation of husband and wife which starts for everyone in 1990 and possibly the separate application of the tax *age allowance* limits on retirement.

Age allowance is an extra personal tax allowance which is given to people over 65 on small incomes so that they pay less income tax on their incomes. From 6 April 1990 both a husband and wife will be entitled to age allowance on their own income which are to be separately taxed from that date. The income limit for age allowance is currently £10,600 – and if you are each entitled to it, your joint pensions of £21,200, provided they are split equally, can give you each an age allowance instead of the normal tax allowances which others have. That means one of you gets one single age allowance of £3,180 instead of the normal £2,605 single allowance and the other gets the married age allowance of £5,035 instead of the usual married allowance of £4,095. The extra age allowances are £1,515 greater than the normal tax allowances which at a 25% basic tax rate saves you £378.75 a year in income tax.

Which type of job pension

If you already have a job pension which just you and your wife belong to it will probably be *money purchase* which means that the benefits depend on what you contribute and the performance of the investment fund or funds in which your contributions are invested or the bonuses it gives if it is a *with-profits* pension. This structure is explained **Chapter 8 How your money grows**.

If you don't already have a pension scheme you should be considering a *director's job pension* also known as a *top hat pension* or an *executive pension*. These have names like Director's Retirement Plan, Executive Retirement Plan, Director Finance Account, Individual Pension Plan. The minimum you can contribute into these schemes ranges from £20 to £60 a month or £200 to £500 a year per person; the minimum lump sum you can contribute ranges from £1,000 to £5,000.

To decide which director's job pension you are going to take you should consult an experienced specialist pensions adviser. If you want to do your own research you should get hold of a copy of the latest edition of *Executive Pensions* by David Lewis published by FT Business Information Ltd which analyses all the different schemes. The book is costly, around £25, and is brought out in new editions every year. It is aimed at financial advisers but is also designed to be read by company directors. How to assess the individual pensions companies and how to choose between them is also considered in **Chapter 12 Which pension company?**

Since 6 April 1988 money purchase job pensions can be *contracted-out* of the State earnings related (additional) pension. To decide whether you should *contract-out* you should read **Chapter 6 If you are an employee without a pension**. The decision for you as a company director is exactly the same as for an employee. The only difference is that if you already have a money purchase job pension, you must check whether your pensions company will allow the scheme to be contracted-out.

If you already have a pension scheme for employees or are considering setting one up you should also read **Chapter 11 If you employ people**.

11
If you employ people

If you are a company director or self-employed and you employ other people in the business you should consider whether your staff as well as yourself should have a pension scheme.

This chapter is mainly concerned with small to medium sized businesses which are fully or mainly owned and run by their directors. Where your company is part of a large group of companies there is often a *group pension scheme* which employees from all the companies can belong. If you are a director of an organisation which does not have shareholders like a charity or building society you will also find this chapter useful.

This chapter first of all considers the position of a company which has no pension scheme at the moment and then goes on to consider whether any changes should be made to an existing pension scheme.

If you run your business as a company you can normally belong to the same pension scheme as your staff although you may wish to arrange an *executive pension* or *top hat pension* with extra benefits as well. If you run your business as a partnership or sole trader, you cannot belong to the same staff pension as your staff – you are only eligible for a personal pension.

Should you offer a pension?

You don't have to offer employees a *staff pension* – and you can choose which employees you want to give a pension to. Since 6 April 1988, you cannot compel employees to belong to a staff pension. Some young employees under age 30 may not want to join; older employees over the age of 40 are more likely to want to join and to appreciate it. In between who knows? If an employee leaves to get a new job and has been in the pension scheme he or she can in most cases transfer the benefits to a new scheme at the new job or into a personal pension.

The cost of a staff pension scheme comes out of the profits of the company. The contributions you as an employer make towards a pension scheme are normally from your profits so they should be regarded as additional costs of employing staff. You get tax relief (income tax if you are self-employed or in a partnership, corporation tax if you have a company) on contributions you make to a job pension just like you get tax relief on the wages and salary you pay your staff. For staff you want to keep, offering a pension is a valuable way of obtaining a commitment to your firm – for trainees and youngsters who you know will not stay with you for long, they are a waste of money. If your staff have children or other dependants your staff can take out life insurance to cover themselves in case they are killed in an accident.

A pensions adviser or pensions company will provide all the documentation in order to set up a new job pension scheme. But you will have to appoint at least one other *trustee* as well as yourself. There will have to be formal meetings regarding decisions on the pension scheme and your pensions company will have to get the scheme approved by the Inland Revenue. You will also have to devote time and trouble to setting up the scheme. You cannot start getting tax relief on the contributions until the Inland Revenue has approved the scheme and the Inland Revenue is not a fast moving organisation.

Non-contributory?

Your older staff may well welcome the introduction of a job pension scheme. They may not be quite so keen on contributing to it. On the other hand a non-contributory pension is a heavy burden for a small business to take on for staff. If staff agree to a contributory scheme, it is an indication that they appreciate it.

However if staff agree to the introduction of a pension scheme instead of a pay rise, there is a saving in national insurance contributions for you as an employer (and usually for the employee too).

Where the pension is *contracted-in* to the State earnings related (additional) pension the saving in employer's national insurance is 10.45% but assuming your company pays corporation tax at 25% after tax relief it is 7.84%; for the employee it is usually 9%. So instead of giving an employee a 5% rise, paying £500 gross but £455 after national insurance, you could offer at the same cost to yourself £500 plus the saving in national insurance contributions of 7.84% of £500 which is £39.19. So you could pay £539.19 as an employer's contribution to a pension scheme at the same cost to you as giving a pay rise which is worth £455 to the employee. The employee then has a pension fund with £84.19 more in it than if he took his own personal pension and you have not increased your costs. Not all employees will appreciate this arithmetic – especially those who want to spend the pay rise rather than put it into a pension.

The result is that if employees agree to a non-contributory pension instead of a pay rise, they can get significantly more in their pension fund than if they had a personal pension at no extra cost to you the employer.

Contract-out or in?

It is your decision as an employer on whether your staff pension scheme should *contract-out* of the State earnings related (additional) pension. However if a member of staff does not like your decision he or she is entitled to refuse to join – or to leave an existing scheme.

Some pension companies have devised an administrative system which can cope with two groups of employees: one pension for those who want to leave the State earnings related (additional) pension and the other for those who want to stay in. That may involve the pension scheme in higher charges.

By making the staff pension contracted-out you will be giving the staff an illusion that they are getting a better deal at any age because in addition to the contributions you make, you can also show how the staff are benefiting from the *rebate* of national insurance contributions and the *incentive* which are paid in to the pension fund as well. These contributions from the State are of course at the expense of the State earnings related (additional) pension.

If you decide to let your staff make their own choice about whether they should contract-out or not, or you choose to make your staff pension contracted-out and you have some employees who decide not to join the pension scheme (or you don't want them to belong), then you will have to cope with two separate scales of deduction for national insurance contributions: contracted-out for those in your staff pension and contracted-in for those who are not. These two scales apply even if the employees who don't join have decided to take a personal pension which is contracted-out because you as an employer still have to use the contracted-in rate of national insurance in such cases; the Department of Health and Social Security hands on the contributions to the pensions company later.

You, the employer, will have less administration if you decide your staff pension is to remain contracted-in to the State earnings related (additional) pension.

It is possible that by setting up a staff pension you may discourage staff from joining a personal pension.

Table 12
National insurance contributions for 1988–89

Yearly earnings £	Employees' contributions Contracted- In %	Out %	Reduced rate %	Employer's contributions Contracted- In %	Out %
2,132 to 3,369	5	3	3.85	5	1.2
3,370 to 5,459	7	5	3.85	7	3.2
5,460 to 8,059	9	7	3.85	9	5.2
8,060 to 15,860	9	7	3.85	10.45	6.65
Over 15,860	On first £15,860 only			10.45	10.45

Contracted out rates apply only to earnings in the band between £2,132 and £15,860. Earnings below £2,132 and over £15,860 (employer only) are at the contracted in rate. If earnings less than £2,132 then no contributions required. Reduced rate applies to some married women only, see Chapter 4 The State pension.

Money purchase or final salary

With a *money purchase* pension, money put in the fund from contributions from employee, employer and (if the scheme is contracted-out) from redirected national insurance contributions is invested in a fund and grows with interest and capital gains on investments. On retirement it is used to buy a pension annuity from an insurance company which gives a pension for life. So the pension depends directly on the amount of contributions and the investment performance – it is not linked to the employee's earnings.

With a *final salary* pension the pension is worked out in terms of a fraction of each employee's earnings, say 1/60th for each year in the scheme. If the regular contributions or the growth in value of the pension fund are not great enough to accumulate a large enough pension fund at retirement, then the employer usually makes it up.

On the other hand if the investment managers who run the pension fund are skillful or lucky or both and investments in the final salary pension fund do particularly well, then the pension fund is in *surplus*. There is more than enough money to pay the pension of your staff and the surplus can be paid to the employer if the documents allow it and subject to a 40% tax payment and the Inland Revenue agrees.

The *trustees*, the people responsible for the pension scheme, have to obtain regular *actuarial estimates* (ie mathematical forecasts made by specialists called actuaries) of the amount of money required to pay for the pensions of staff who are members of a final salary pension. If the investments are doing very well, you the employer, can for a time take a *pensions holiday*; that means you can stop making contributions for as long as the scheme remains in surplus.

If the investments perform poorly, then the company may feel obliged to make extra contributions to top up the pension fund. That happens not only at the time staff are due to retire, but at any time when the actuarial estimates state there will be a shortfall. The extra you pay is usually not a lump sum but merely an increase in the rate at which you pay into the pension fund – say from 12% a year of your staff's salary bill to 14% a year.

My own feeling is that a final salary pension is not really a good idea for a small business particularly now that younger employees can decide not to join and have a right to a transfer value when they leave. The result may be very expensive if only older employees decide to join or remain in the pension scheme.

Simplified job pension

This is a new type of job pension scheme which is easier for an employer to set up. There is less hassle with the Inland Revenue which basically rubber stamps a standard set of documents.

It works more like a personal pension rather than other types of job pension. The main point in its favour compared with a personal pension is that if it is fully non-contributory, and the employee agrees to lower pay or to forego a pay rise in return, it can save the employer and employee national insurance contributions compared with the same money going into a personal pension.

Money purchase

Where the simplified scheme is on a *money purchase* basis the rules are virtually the same as a personal pension though contributions to a *simplified job pension* are restricted to 17.5% of an employee's earnings (with a maximum of 15% paid by the employee) and no extra contributions are allowed for the over 50's. The scheme may be contracted-out of the State earnings related (additional) pension but if it is, the 17.5% limit includes the redirected rebate of national insurance contributions.

Members of a simplified job pension are allowed to make *free standing additional voluntary contributions* and ordinary *additional voluntary contributions* if you, the employer, set up a scheme. Additional voluntary contributions must also be within the 15% and 17.5% limits.

Retirement is between ages 50 and 70 (not 75 like a personal pension) – and there doesn't have to be a fixed retirement age as there is with other types of job pension.

But if the pension is contracted-out of the State earnings related (additional) pension then the part of the pension accumulated from the redirection of national insurance contributions cannot start before age 60 for women, 65 for men.

There are no restrictions on the amount of pension which can be taken at retirement – and the cash lump sum is based on 25% of the accumulated pension fund like a personal pension (with a maximum of £150,00).

However if you decide to make the simplified job pension one which is contracted-out of the State earnings related (additional) pension, you pay national insurance contributions for your staff at the contracted-out rate as with an ordinary staff pension. This is an advantage for the staff who belong to the *simplified job pension* compared with a *personal pension* as you pay the rebate of national insurance contributions to their pension company for investment each month instead of them having to wait until at least three months after the end of the tax year for the Department of Health and Social Security to hand the money over to the pensions company.

The disadvantage of a simplified job pension for an employer compared with a personal pension is that because of the way contracted-out national insurance contributions are sent to pensions companies, you as an employer will probably have to cope with two sets of deductions for national insurance as you would have to with an ordinary job pension.

Final salary

It is also possible to have a *simplified final salary* pension scheme where the rules are slightly different. Employer's contributions are unlimited. But benefits are restricted and a pension of two thirds final salary can only build up with 40 years service for the company compared with 20 years under an ordinary final salary job pension. Otherwise the rules are similar to the money purchase version.

Group personal pensions

Group personal pensions are where an employer asks a pensions company to offer personal pensions to his staff as a group. Contributions are collected by deduction from each employee's wages or salary. But each employee has an individual personal pension which belongs to him and he can continue with if he or she moves jobs.

An employer can also make contributions to each employee's personal pension which are paid together with the employee's contributions. Employers' contributions don't count as part of your employee's salary so there is a saving in national insurance contributions as there is with employers' contributions to a job pension. The rules for group personal pensions are otherwise exactly the same as for personal pensions. Employees can decide for themselves whether they want to be contracted-out of the State earning related (additional) pension. If they do decide to opt out that makes no difference to the national insurance contributions you as an employer pay for them which remain the same for all employees at the contracted-in rate.

Employers have to fill in forms for employees who take out personal pensions regarding their employment. With a group personal pension the information for all employees can be collected together and sent off together to the one pensions company dealing with the group scheme.

In order to discourage employees taking out their own personal pension, employers who set up group personal pensions will probably need to make contributions themselves or choose a company which has significantly lower charges for its pensions. Otherwise employees may decide they can do better with another pensions company.

Existing job pensions

If you already run a job pension for your employees which you are satisifed with, there is no particular reason to change it. Remember that job pensions which people joined before 17 March 1987 can have higher lump sums and higher pensions built up over a shorter number of years than job pensions started after that date which is a good reason to stick with the original scheme if you contemplate giving some staff extra benefits at some stage in the future. It should be possible to improve the old scheme without jeopardising the tax position but you should get expert advice on this point before you make any changes in the rules. Extra benefits as a result of extra contributions to a money purchase scheme should not affect the limits on retirement.

New employees who join the scheme now are subject to the new more restrictive rules.

Let employees do their own thing

You don't have to set up a pension scheme for employees. If most of your staff are young, under 30 say, don't. You can make an arrangement with an individual life and pensions adviser or, say, two life and pensions companies who can supply quotes to any employees who are interested in a personal pension or life insurance. Provided you get good advice on the choice of company you might save the employee falling into the clutches of a pensions salesman who knocks on the door or phones up out of the blue.

12
Which pensions company?

Not all pensions companies offer all the different types of pensions or options described in this book. Your first step towards a pension, whether you are an individual employee, self-employed or an employer is to work out which type of pension is best for your own individual circumstances. Only when you have done that should you start to choose between individual pensions companies.

However that advice is a bit theoretical because most of the advice and information available on pensions comes from individual pensions companies themselves. Independent pensions advisers often depend on the pensions companies for the technical information they supply you. And the leaflets and booklets from individual companies may help you choose the best type of pension for you. If you don't find the explanatory information easily understandable, try another pensions company. Some pensions companies are much better than others at explaining things.

Independent financial advice

At all levels it is essential to get unbiased advice on pensions. At the very least make sure your pensions adviser is either a member of *FIMBRA* or an *insurance broker* (ie registered by the Insurance Brokers' Registration Council) or is a firm of *consulting actuaries*.

If you are setting up a *staff pension* or a *director's or executive pension* it is essential that the pensions adviser has some proven experience as a specialist pensions consultant; ask for the names of two customers as references and phone them for their views on the pensions consultant.

The advice you get on pensions may vary depending on how the adviser is paid. In most cases the adviser is paid by commission. The other method is to pay the adviser a fee for work done. An increased investment allocation can be given if the adviser reduces his commission.

If your pensions adviser is paid by commission, he has an incentive to persuade you to pay the highest possible contributions as his commission is linked to what you pay. It is also possible that some types of pensions pay higher commission than other types; some pensions companies pay higher commission than others; and a few pay none at all.

An independent pensions adviser should not take the amount of commission he receives into account when recommending you a pension which is supposed to be based on objective criteria. This rule could cause great difficulties for independent advisers if there happens to be a 'best' company by objective criteria which pays no commission, or lower commission than its competitors. Theoretically the adviser should sacrifice his commission for the good of the customer or charge a fee. Unfortunately there is rarely a completely objective criteria for choosing a particular pension or a particular pensions company.

That is why the Life Assurance and Unit Trust Regulatory Organisation (known as LAUTRO) for the main pensions companies has proposed a system of maximum commission rates in order to save pensions advisers from needing to be altruistic. All companies which pay commission are likely to pay the maximum rate. The commission rate rules have been criticised as being anti-competitive and at the time of writing it is not certain whether they will be enforced. Even if they are not it is still likely that most pensions companies will pay the same commission rate – it is the few, if any, that pay over the odds which you should be wary of.

Comparative surveys

Once you have decided which type of pension is right for you it may be useful to read up on it yourself. You will then have a yardstick with which to judge the advice that your pensions adviser gives you. Three magazines which publish surveys which are likely to be understandable to non-technical people are *Which?* magazine published by Consumers Association Ltd on subscription only; and with more regular surveys *Money Management* and *Pensions Management* magazines both published by Financial Times Business Information Ltd. Single copies are available of both of these magazines, back issues from the publishers and current issues through newsagents.

Financial Times Business Information Ltd also publishes a series of guide books for professional advisers which give a lot of detail on each of the individual pensions companies' schemes. New editions of these are planned for the Autumn of 1988. They are *Personal Pensions 1988–89, Executive Pensions 1988–89* and a new title called *Additional Voluntary Contributions.* As these guides cost around £25 each it might be an idea to ask your local public library to get a copy. Meanwhile the current edition of *Executive Pensions 1987–88* by David Lewis which includes pensions for company directors is still applicable. Another book in the same series *Self-*

Employed Pensions 1987–88 by Janet Walford gives details of retirement annuities available from life insurance companies and was published at the beginning of 1988; many of the retirement annuities surveyed in that book will be similar to personal pensions now available though you can now only add to an existing retirement annuity, you cannot start a new plan.

The basis for comparing

The way in which you can decide on competing products depends partly on the type you choose. In **Chapter 8 How your money grows** there is a description of many different ways in which the money you contribute to all types of pensions accumulates. What you have to compare varies according to type of investment you have chosen. If you get hold of the comparative surveys in the books and magazines recommended above you will see that the surveys are of different things.

Past performance

Good past performance is often put forward as a reason for linking a pension to a particular fund. Unfortunately there is no evidence to show that good performance of an *investment linked pension fund* over one or more years in the past will mean that that fund will be good or best in the future. In fact when it comes to funds invested in stocks and shares, the reverse can be the case. The very best performing funds over a short period, say 12 months, tend to be invested in *volatile* shares which rise most when the stock market is going up, and fall furthest when it is going down (and then the fund manager gets fired and they never recover!).

Past performance of a *with-profits* type pension is a better guide to the future provided the method by which the profits are added to the pension fund has not altered. Many pensions companies are changing the way in which they add bonuses to pension funds with the introduction of personal pensions and the new funds may not be comparable to the old ones. There is no doubt that the companies which are top of the tables with with-profits pensions are much more consistent than those with investment linked pensions.

Unfortunately the trend is to more emphasis on bonuses which are added on retirement which makes with-profits more like investment linked pension funds and more liable to year by year fluctuations in the results. This is covered in detail in **Chapter 8 How your money grows**.

Charges

The charges made by a pensions company depend on the way in which the pension fund benefits are accumulated. The different types are explained in Chapter 8. With *deposit based* and *guaranteed or non profit* pension funds there are normally no explicit charges – the interest rate given is after deduction of any charges.

The same can apply to *with-profits* pension funds. However increasingly new types of with-profits funds have charges before your money is invested in the pension fund. No one has yet decided the best way to analyse these charges.

With *investment linked* pension funds the charges are deducted to a variety of different ways. It is possible to assess these charges by making projections of future accumulated pension funds at common assumed rates of growth and after deduction of all charges. Pensions companies are unfortunately prohibited by LAUTRO or the Securities and Investment Board from supplying projections based on their own actual charges. Any they supply must be based on a fixed formula which shows all companies as projecting virtually the same amounts.

Projections on a standard basis can be made by magazines and in books and are included in the more useful of the comparative surveys recommended above. If you are considering an investment linked pension, your first decision should be to select a group of pensions companies which have relatively low charges. The higher charging companies are less likely to be companies which seek their business through independent advisers and are more likely to be those which sell direct to the public through teams of salesmen.

A process of elimination

With so much competition for pensions of all types there is not likely to be any clear cut 'best buy'. Choosing the right pension is likely to be a process of elimination. With the help of your pensions adviser, if you have one, and using the comparative surveys, if you can be bothered, choose in this order:

1. The type of pension or pensions which are most suited to you. Firstly choose between a *personal pension* and a *job pension* if this is applicable.

2. If you are an employee and choose a job pension, should you make *additional voluntary contributions?* If the answer is yes, decide whether you should go for the scheme offered by your employer or to a *free standing additional voluntary contributions* scheme with a pensions company of your own choice.

3. Having decided on which type of pension scheme is best for you unless you belong to a *final salary job pension* you will probably have to decide which type of invest-

ments you want your pension fund invested in. If you are in a job scheme you could leave it to your employer to decide instead. Choose the type of investment linking or with-profits which suits you best.

4. With a *personal pension* or a *free standing additional voluntary contributions* pension find out which companies have the lowest charges. From these find out which have had the best performance for the type of fund which you want to invest in over the past five years.

5. Finally consider leaving out of your list the small new pensions companies which are not long established or which are foreign owned or are likely to be the victim of a takeover bid. If your pensions company is taken over you are not likely to be happy with the change of management. The takeover may be the result of a bid on the stockmarket or merely because the owner of a pensions company, often a foreign owner, finds the profits of the pensions company are not as great as he expected when he bought or set it up.

13
Changing jobs

One of the main reasons for all the changes in the rules for pensions is the aim to improve matters for people who change jobs. The detailed rules are very complex because they are designed to avoid abuse of the generous tax rules which all pension schemes have. Most pensions can now be transferred to any other pension. In practice Inland Revenue rules may make some transfers impracticable – but these restrictions will only affect a minority of people, particularly directors who own and work for their own company.

When you make a transfer from one type of pension scheme to another you do not get any more tax relief, nor do you have to pay any tax on the transfer value.

Job pension transfers

Since 6 April 1988 job pensions are no longer compulsory. Before that date it was unusual, though not impossible, to leave a job pension unless you also left the employment of the firm which ran the pension scheme. You can now also sometimes transfer your accumulated pension fund from a job pension to another sort of pension without leaving your employment. However if you are not leaving the firm

it is not necessarily advisable to leave your job pension –
whether you should or not is covered in **Chapter 6 If you
are already in a job pension**.

You have only had the right to transfer your accumulated pension fund from a job pension since 1 January
1986 although many employers allowed transfers before
that date. If you leave the pension scheme but not the
service of the employer, you can only transfer benefits
earned after 6 April 1988; the rest has to wait until you
leave the service of that employer.

The transfer value from the job pension you are leaving
has to be based on your *preserved pension*. Your preserved
pension is the pension you would get from the old job
pension at the normal retirement date for that pension
scheme.

The transfer value will be the present value of your
preserved pension with all the appropriate increases
subject to a minimum of the amount you have made in
contributions yourself. Depending on how much you have
contributed if you are over the age of 35 or so it is likely to
be more – and the older you are the greater it is.

From a final salary pension

With a *final salary* pension scheme it is relatively simple
to work out. Your final salary might be the salary in your
last full year before you leave. Suppose your final salary
pension scheme is based on so many 1/60ths for each year
you have been in the pension scheme. And suppose you
have been with the company ten years. Then your
preserved pension is 10/60ths of your salary when you
leave.

With a salary of £10,000, then your preserved pension
is 10/60ths of £10,000 which is £1,667. But what about
inflation? Suppose you are 55 now and the normal
retirement age is 65. Look up the value of £1,000 in ten

years time in the tables in Appendix 3 at the back of the book assuming inflation averages 3% a year. It is £744. For £10,000 multiply by ten to give £7,440. So your pension in ten years time in today's money will only really be worth 10/60ths of £7,440 which is £1,240 unless some adjustment for inflation is made.

Some job pensions *revalue* the whole of the preserved pension of a job leaver. But apart from the part of the pension which is instead of the State earnings related (additional) pension (called the *guaranteed minimum pension* or *GMP*), job pensions are only compelled to revalue preserved pensions for pensions earned (ie for periods which you belonged to the pension scheme) after 1 January 1985 and up to the increase of retail prices in each full calendar year with a maximum of 5% in any year.

In the example above assuming your company only did what it is obliged to do by law and no more, then possibly three of your ten year's membership would be revalued.

So your pension would be 7/60ths of £10,000 which is £1,167. Plus 3/60ths of £10,000 *revalued* by prices. Looking at the table in Appendix 1 you can see that £1,000 at 3% a year grows to £1,344. So £10,000 grows to £13,440. So 3/60ths of £13,440 is £672. Add that to £1,167 and you have a total pension of £1,839.

To work out what that is worth in today's money you look again at Appendix 3 and find that £10,000 in ten years time with 3% a year inflation is worth £7,441. You then multiply £1,839 by £7,441 and divide the answer by £10,000 to get the result which is £1,368.

So by leaving your pension as a *preserved pension* you have 'lost' the difference between £1,368 and £1,667 a year of your pension. That is £299 a year. You have probably lost more than this because had you stayed with the firm and in the old pension scheme, your earnings would probably have grown at a greater rate than prices, so your final salary (and therefore your pension) if you stayed would be larger than the revalued amount of your leaving salary even if it was entirely revalued for price increases. Of course when you leave for a new job you get an immediate pay rise and better prospects.

The closer you are to retirement age, the less adviseable is it to leave or transfer from a final salary job pension unless you are transferring into another final salary job pension – see below.

From a money purchase job pension

With a money purchase job pension as your benefits are based on the amount accumulated in your individual pension fund, you are usually entitled to the value of your accumulated pension fund which should include employer's as well as employee's contributions. However the detailed rules for transfers may result in a transfer value if you are young which is no more than the value of your own contributions or alternatively to the value of the accumulated pension fund based on your own contributions only.

A *preserved pension* with a money purchase job pension should be worth the same amount as the transfer value. It will continue to grow in line with the fund in which it is invested. Whether you wish to transfer depends entirely on whether you think the *pension fund* you plan to transfer to will perform better than the one to which you already belong. That is virtually impossible to predict – though you may feel that leaving the old job pension and transferring to a personal pension gives you more control over your own money.

From a contracted-out job pension

There can be some more complications if you want to

transfer from a job pension which is *contracted-out* of the State earnings related (additional) pension to one which is not. In the past this was not possible. One option now is for some of your transfer value to be used to *buy you back* into the State earnings related (additional) pension. Your old pension scheme will arrange this for you.

To a final salary job pension

If you move jobs from a firm with a final salary job pension to a new firm with a final salary job pension and you are over the age of 35 to 40 you should try and ensure that the company agrees to accept your transfer on a *years for years* basis. So if you are leaving the old scheme with ten year's pension accumulated, you should ask your new employer to take you into the new pension scheme as if you have already paid for ten years. That way you do not lose out though it could be expensive for your employer.

However as in this example seven of the ten years were before 1 January 1985 and do not have to be revalued, your new firm's job pension will say there is not enough money in the transfer value to pay for ten years in the new job pension at an as yet unknown future final salary. They may offer you say seven or five years instead. Another reason for a transfer value not being enough to give you a transfer on a years for years basis is that you are likely to be earning more in the new job than in the old job. Your transfer value will be based on your old final salary in the old job plus revaluation. Whereas in the new job your final salary, on which they work out the cost of paying for your pension, will be based on your new higher salary. If there is any difference, then the transfer value will be too small to allow a years for years transfer.

You must realise that a job pension is separate from the new firm you are joining. If your new employer says: "Of course the pension scheme will give you full credit for pension earned from your transfer value" be careful. It is the trustees of the job pension who must decide how to accept a transfer and how much credit to give you for it. If they are advised that there is not enough money in your transfer value, then they need to get the money from somewhere. You therefore need an explicit agreement from your new employer as part of your contract of employment or job offer that the job pension will accept your transfer value and if there is not enough money to give you a full years for years transfer then the new firm will make a special contribution to make up any shortfall.

It will be too late if you find this out after you have joined. The time to negotiate is after you have been offered the job and when your salary has been agreed.

To a money purchase job pension

A transfer from a money purchase job pension to a money purchase job pension with a new job should present no difficulties. However there could be a charge made on a transfer by the pensions company of the scheme you are leaving which would not apply if you kept a *preserved pension*. You will have to make your own enquiries. There is no point in transferring from a final salary job pension with your old employer to a money purchase job pension with your new employer – if you don't want a preserved pension, transfer to a *personal pension* where you have complete control over your money or to a *section 32 buy out bond* which are described below.

To a personal pension

The new rules allow you to make transfers from a job pension to a personal pension. There are some restrictions on this for high earners and *controlling directors*, that is people who own more than 20% of the company which they work for (and have done so in the past ten years). The rules are intended to avoid abuse of the rules which restrict a job pension to a proportion of your final salary in the company while personal pensions have no restrictions on pensions, only on contributions.

To a buy out bond

As an alternative to a transfer to a personal pension, you can transfer instead to another type of individual pension called a *buy out bond* or a *Section 32 buy out bond*. This is a special type of individual pension fund where you can transfer the value of your pension rights from a job pension. The money accumulates tax free in the buy out bond until you retire, normally between ages 60 and 70 at the retirement date from your original job pension. When you retire you get a pension and you may be able to take part of the accumulated pension fund as a lump sum instead of part of your pension.

The benefits are based on the benefits given by the job pension which you have transferred from. The pensions company (normally a life insurance company) which offers the buy out bond has to get detailed information from your old job pension which can make negotiating a transfer a lengthy business. The minimum transfer depends on the pensions company which runs the buy out bond and is usually £1,000 to £2,000.

Otherwise the buy out bond works in a similar way to a personal pension with a choice of different investments and charges and a refund of the value of the fund or contribution plus interest if you die before retirement. You cannot add contributions to a buy out bond but you can transfer later to a job pension or a personal pension.

Personal pension transfers

I can see no benefit in transferring from a personal pension to a job pension. You are allowed to transfer from a personal pension with one pensions company to one with another pensions company. This will not normally be worth doing, unless the performance is very bad, because the original pensions company is likely to deduct a charge if you do which should be incentive enough for you to remain. You cannot transfer from a personal pension to a *retirement annuity* or to a *buy out bond*.

Retirement annuity transfers

One reason for transferring from a retirement annuity into a personal pension is when you want to use the *open market option* to enable you to get a better *pension annuity* just before you retire from a life company other than the one which you have had your pension scheme with up till then. **Chapter 3 How pensions work** explains how the maximum cash lump sum allowed on a retirement annuity is generally larger than that allowed for a personal pension. So normally using the open market option is not a good idea.

However you can transfer to another retirement annuity provided you already have a policy and the existing company agrees.

For most people the minimum retirement age with a retirement annuity is 60 whereas for an ordinary personal pension it is 50. If you want to start drawing your pension earlier than 60 then you should transfer from a retirement annuity to a personal pension.

Generally speaking if you transfer from a retirement annuity to a personal pension with the same life insurance company there will be no extra charge. However if you want to transfer to another pensions company (except when you are using the open market option) there will be a charge so it is best to stay with the original company.

Refund of contributions

You can receive a refund of your contributions to a job pension if you leave employment and have been in it for less than two years. Any refund has a special 20% tax rate deducted from it. You can get a refund if you leave the pension scheme within two years but do not leave the organisation you are working for. You cannot receive a refund of contributions from a personal pension or a retirement annuity. But with a personal pension on retirement, if the value of the pension you would get is *trivial*, that is under £104 a year, you are allowed to take the whole of your pension fund as a lump sum on retirement.

14
Life insurance with tax relief

With a job pension you can get life insurance as well as a pension. The insurance pays out a fixed sum, usually a multiple of your pensionable earnings. So if you are earning £10,000 then your job pension may pay £10,000 to £40,000 to your widow or a named dependant if you die while you are working before you retire.

The maximum amount that can be paid is four times your earnings – but this can be in addition to any widow's pension you get from the job pension.

Do it yourself

If you are not in a job pension you can take out life insurance yourself as a separate type of personal pension policy from a life insurance company. Instead of paying a pension, the policy pays out a tax free lump sum – or a tax free income to your dependants – if you die before the age which you choose the policy to last for. The policy has to end when you are age 75. The premiums to this type of policy cannot exceed 5% of your earnings and come within the 17.5% (more if you are over 50) limit for personal pensions. If you want to pay the maximum amount you are allowed to into a personal pension, it is better to take one of these insurance policies as an ordinary policy without the tax relief on the premiums so you can use your full contribution limit towards a pension.

If you are in a job pension which does not give life insurance benefits you cannot take out one of these special policies but you can have ordinary life insurance.

The cost

The cost of the premiums you pay depends on how much life insurance you want, your age when you start, whether you are a man or a woman and with many companies whether you smoke cigarettes. These types of policies are relatively cheap, especially when you are younger. They are similar to ordinary types of life insurance which are called *term insurance, increasing term insurance*, and a few companies also offer *family income benefit* and *mortgage protection*.

Term insurance

This pays a lump sum if you die within a certain term which you choose at the outset and during which you pay monthly or yearly premiums. You might want to choose the term to end when your children grow up or go on to the maximum to age 75.

Increasing term insurance

This is the same as term insurance except that the lump sum paid if you die is raised regularly, either every year, or every three or five years. The premiums rise as the increase in insurance cover. These policies are often in the form of 3 or 5 year policies which have an option to take a larger policy every three or five years. A few companies link premiums and cover to the index of retail prices.

Normally increasing policies end at age 60 or 65 or if they last longer, you can't get any guaranteed increases after these ages.

Family income benefit

Family income benefit pays a regular income monthly, quarterly, half-yearly or yearly after your death to your widow, widower or dependants. You choose the term, that is how long you want the income to be paid (eg 15 years or until your youngest child is 18 or 21) and you pay premiums until then. Equitable Life has a version which is slightly more costly which continues to pay the income until you would have been age 100.

Increasing family income benefit

This is just like family income benefit except that the income once it starts to be paid rises each year by say 5% a year. Generally the premiums don't rise over the term, so this policy is a lot more expensive than ordinary family income benefit.

Mortgage protection

Also known as *decreasing term insurance*, this pays a lump sum designed to pay off the outstanding loan of a repayment mortgage often at a stated interest rate on the mortgage. Some life insurance companies offer policies which will pay off the loan whatever the interest rate. But if you are making regular contributions to a personal pension you should instead consider a *pension mortgage* (see **Chapter 15 Mortgages and loan backs**) in which case you will be asked to take a *term insurance* policy instead of a *mortgage protection* policy.

Tax relief on life insurance

These special life insurance policies get tax relief at your highest tax rate. If you are an employee or company director you get allowed the basic tax rate in the premium you pay. So if the premium is £10, the life company will usually ask you to pay £7.50 while the basic tax rate remains at 25%. If you pay at 40% then you get the extra 15% tax relief, £1.50 in this case, later in your tax assessment. If you are self-employed, you get all the tax relief in your tax assessment.

The premiums you can pay to these policies are worked out in the same way as the contributions you pay to a personal pension. But instead of the 17.5% allowance (and more if you are over 50) the maximum you can pay is 5% of earnings. The 5% is part of the 17.5% – so if you are already using up all your allowance with a pension, you cannot take any extra life insurance.

If you join a job pension

If you join a job pension, you have to stop paying premiums to one of these special life insurance policies unless you have a second job or earnings from part time self-employment which give you enough allowances to qualify. However most life insurance companies offer you an option to convert your special life insurance policy to an ordinary one with the same benefits and premiums and no need to give health evidence. The proceeds of these ordinary life insurance policies are also exempt from tax.

Probate and inheritance tax

If you die early you can avoid hassle for your relatives by asking the pensions company to make the proceeds of any

le 13

e monthly cost before tax relief of £50,000 term
urance

| Length of policy | | | | | To age 65 | To age 75 |
10 yrs £	15 yrs £	20 yrs £	25 yrs £	30 yrs £	£	£
5.00	5.00	5.14	5.66	6.36	8.24	10.21
5.01	5.49	6.27	7.32	8.64	10.13	13.10
6.54	7.72	9.29	11.26	13.45	13.45	17.91
10.17	12.49	15.29	18.48	21.85	18.48	25.09
16.95	21.02	25.61	30.51	35.28	25.61	35.28
28.33	35.15	42.19	49.24	–	35.15	49.24
46.44	57.29	67.66	–	–	46.44	67.66
74.18	90.80	–	–	–	51.25	90.80
115.43	–	–	–	–	–	115.43
–	–	–	–	–	–	114.56

man

5.00	5.00	5.09	5.40	5.84	7.15	8.73
5.00	5.00	5.40	6.10	7.06	8.11	10.52
5.40	6.14	7.19	8.59	10.21	10.21	13.76
7.67	9.25	11.26	13.67	16.29	13.67	18.96
12.44	15.38	18.79	22.59	26.53	18.79	26.53
20.84	25.88	31.34	37.08	–	25.88	37.08
34.63	42.85	51.12	–	–	34.63	51.12
56.19	69.10	–	–	–	39.53	69.10
88.83	–	–	–	–	–	88.83
–	–	–	–	–	–	90.84

smoker rates. Age next birthday. Source: Norwich Union.

life insurance you have payable direct to your widow,
widower or dependants. By doing this the life insurance
company pays the money straightaway to the person you

have nominated and payment of the money does not have wait until your *will* (or the money you have left if you have not made a will) has gone through *probate* where it is cleared by a special government department. Probate can take from three months to over a year; it is usually much quicker if your widow or widower does it themselves.

Banks and solicitors often base their charges for dealing with probate on the size of your *estate*, the money or property left to you. Your widow or widower can save money on the bank or solicitor's bill when you let the proceeds of a life insurance company come direct to him or her rather than being part of your estate.

With a job pension, your employer has discretion on who to pay the money to but generally asks you to fill in a form which asks you what you want.

With a personal pension life policy you have to fill in a trust form which you can get from the insurance company. These trust forms usually appoint your wife or husband, or the executors of your will if you wish, as the trustee or trustees to whom the life insurance company pays the money. You can also specify who is to receive the money – ie your widow, or if she is not alive your children in equal shares. Or the trust can state that the trustees can make up their own minds within two years of your death in which case you should write them a letter and keep it with your will telling them who they should give the money to.

If your estate when you die comes to more than £110,000 for 1988–89 including the value of your home, then unless you leave it all to a legally married husband or wife 40% of the excess is taken by the Government in *inheritance tax*. The proceeds of any life insurance policy which is in trust falls outside your estate and is therefore not liable to inheritance tax.

If you die early you usually also get a refund of the value of any accumulated pension fund you have paid contributions to (sometimes instead you get back your contributions with or without interest). These contributions may form part of your estate and therefore may be liable to probate and inheritance tax if the estate is. With some personal pensions you pay lower charges in exchange for agreeing not to get anything back if you die before you start to draw the pension.

15
Pension mortgages and loan backs

You can link a pension to a mortgage and as a result make lower payments on your mortgage. That is called a *pension mortgage*. You can also borrow back your contributions from a pension fund, provided you have security, which is called a *loan back*. Pension mortgages and loan backs can be made with certain types of job pensions but they are really much better suited to personal pensions (or retirement annuities if you already have one and especially one to which you are able to pay extra contributions). This chapter confines itself to personal pensions and retirement annuities and unless otherwise stated wherever a personal pension is mentioned the same rules also apply to a retirement annuity. If you want to get a pension mortgage linked to a job pension you should speak to the organisation you are getting a mortgage from.

Pension mortgages

With a pension mortgage you pay interest to the bank, building society or other lender which lends you the money and you also take out two personal pension plans to cover the mortgage. One of the personal pensions is the normal one which you save towards a pension with; the other is a *term insurance* personal pension, described in the previous chapter, which pays off the mortgage if you die early.

You pay enough contributions to the normal personal pension plan so the estimated tax free cash lump sum on your chosen retirement date is large enough to repay the mortgage. The sum insured on the term insurance personal pension is equal to the amount you have borrowed and repays it if you die before retirement.

Your aim should be to choose a retirement date which allows you the minimum contributions to cover the personal pension and the term insurance personal pension. The longer the repayment period, the lower the contributions to the normal personal pension as your money has longer to accumulate interest and gains in your pension fund. But the term insurance personal pension gets more costly the older you are when it ends as there is more risk of you dying. Your retirement date can be between age 50 and 75 so you can end your mortgage at any time between those dates. If you already have a retirement annuity and use that for a pension mortgage then the retirement dates are from age 60 to 75.

There is normally no point in taking a pension mortgage on more than £30,000, or £30,000 each if you are two single people with a joint mortgage and contracts were exchanged and the mortgage offer made before 1 August 1988. That is the limit on which you get tax relief for buying your own home – and if the rest of the loan is larger and is not eligible for tax relief you should try and pay it off as quickly as you can. However if the loan is for a business purpose there can be a point in having a pension mortgage of over £30,000.

Pension mortgages are even more attractive if you pay the higher 40% tax rate and for such taxpayers are likely to be the cheapest way to repay a mortgage except for a *standing mortgage* described below.

Compared with an endowment mortgage

A pension mortgage after tax relief only costs a few pounds a month more than a *low-cost endowment* mortgage. If you are offered a low cost endowment, and are eligible for a personal pension, then ask for a quotation for a personal pension mortgage too and compare them. The lump sum you get after paying off your mortgage may be larger with a low cost endowment but the pension mortgage will almost certainly give you a better deal overall. For a 40% taxpayer the pension mortgage is usually cheaper than a low cost endowment. A pension mortgage is also cheaper than a full endowment mortgage for a basic rate taxpayer.

Compared with a repayment mortgage

A *repayment mortgage* is still usually the cheapest form of mortgage available for basic rate taxpayers. The best type is the *gross profile* or *varying payments* method but unfortunately they are offered only by a few lenders including Lloyds Bank, Midland Bank, National Westminster Bank, Royal Bank of Scotland, TSB, National & Provincial building society and, as an option, by the Halifax and Guardian building societies and Barclays Bank.

Although falling mortgage rates have favoured endowment and pension mortgages, falling tax rates and falling insurance company tax rates have favoured repayment mortgages. Above 7.5% to 8.5% interest before tax relief a repayment mortgage is still cheaper than an endowment and a pension mortgage; whether it is better is still a matter of controversy and depends on what you get back when the endowment or pension policy comes to an end.

Compared with a standing mortgage

Some lenders have so much money to lend that they now allow you to borrow without making repayments of capital nor making you take out an endowment or pension policy from which you will repay the proceeds. They reckon you can repay them when you sell the home, or when you die. In such a case you could just take out a personal pension *term insurance* policy and you would then have the cheapest payments of all. In fact you may not even be required to take out insurance although that is probably a sensible thing to do as the cost is low. Remember that once you reach age 75, the term policy will have ended, but after getting to this age your widow or widower will probably have accumulated a large enough pension to pay the relatively small mortgage payments assuming that inflation will have reduced the real value of the mortgage payment over the years.

Pensions company loan back

With this type of *loan back* you pay contributions to a personal pension, normally a large single contribution, or you have accumulated a large pension fund from regular contributions. You may be able to pay the large single contribution because you are able to use up 17.5% allowances from previous tax years (see Chapter 3 for a full explanation). The pensions company then gives you a loan of up to 100% of your pension fund.

Many pensions companies will not give a loan back which is initially less than £15,001 because they have to issue special documents under the Consumer Credit Act if the loan is £15,000 or below.

To get a loan back you require security, normally a first or second mortgage on property (say your own home or a country cottage or commercial premises) although some pensions companies accept stocks and shares. The loan is *non status*, which means it does not depend on your income but only on the value of the security and your pension fund.

The loan plus any existing mortgage, must be less than around 70% to 80% of the value of the property (less for stocks and shares, say 50%).

You have to pay the cost of the pensions company's valuer – in some cases they let you find your own and pay him direct which might come to 1% of the cost of the property plus 15% VAT. You also have to pay the pensions company's legal costs and the cost of registering the mortgage at the Land Registry. These legal costs might come to about £150 and you should ask for an estimate in advance and don't forget the VAT too. Some pensions companies insist that you pay the extra legal costs every time you increase the loan. Extra valuation costs may not be necessary every time if your original loan was relatively small (say less than 50%) of the first valuation of the property.

How it works

If you are making a personal pension contribution with a loan back in mind it makes life easier if you choose an *investment linked* type of pension scheme.

Suppose you pay a single contribution to a personal pension of £10,000. The company deducts its initial charge of 5% which leaves £9,500 in your pension fund. If you are a 40% higher rate taxpayer you will have received 40% tax relief on your contribution. So the cost to you is £6,000. You can reduce the current cost to nil by taking a loan back for say £6,300. The £6,000 pays you back what you have paid after tax relief as a contribution – and the £300 covers your costs on the transaction.

Having completed the transaction you have a pension fund which is worth £3,200 at an outlay to you of nothing.

Interest need not be paid

The loan back costs you interest though. If you wish, and provided you are below the limits of the loan as a percentage of your security and also as a percentage of your pension fund, you need not pay any interest. Instead the interest is added to the loan. This may not be worth doing if the loan is used for a business purpose in which case you can get tax relief on the interest but only if you pay it.

With a loan back where the interest is accumulated, the amount you owe grows each year. So if you have borrowed £6,300 and the interest charged is 10%, then after a year you will owe £6,300 plus £630 interest which makes £6,930. You can work out what you owe after ten years by looking at **Appendix 1 How money grows: lump sums**. The table shows £1,000 grows to £2,594 after ten years at 10% interest. So to find out how £6,300 grows multiply £2,594 by £6,300 and divide by 1000. The answer is after ten years you will owe £16,342. That is no problem so long as the value of your property is high in relation to the amount of the loan or, as has been the case in the past, the value of your property grows by at least the same amount as the interest you are paying.

If your loan looks as if it is going to exceed the limit of, say, 70% of the value of the property when you started the loan back the pensions company will want the property revalued. In the unlikely event of the revaluation not being high enough you will be asked to start paying the interest until the value of your property is high enough to allow the interest to accumulate.

The value of your pension fund

Your pension fund can be dealt with in one of two ways. Not all companies allow both options.

1. Either you can have your contributions invested in whichever investment fund you have chosen as the most suitable for you – for instance a mixed or managed fund, an equity fund if you think the stockmarket will do well or a fixed interest fund if you are nearer retirement and more cautious. Advice on how these differ is given in **Chapter 8 How your money grows**. The only snag with doing this is that if you make the wrong decision and the investments don't do very well, the value of your pension fund will not grow enough to pay off your loan when you retire. That may not be a problem if you intend to use the proceeds of the sale of the property to pay off the loan back. But remember that the loan back from the pensions company cannot continue after age 75 which is the latest date you can take the pension. And if you have the loan back on the home you live in and don't want to move then your only alternative if you have no other money is to get a new standing loan from a building society to pay off the loan from the pensions company. You will probably have to pay the interest on the new loan.

2. Or you can switch your pension fund into a special deposit fund which pays interest at a rate, usually 1.5% or 2% less than the rate you are paying on the loan. This means that what you owe is always linked to what is accumulating in your pension fund although the longer the loan back lasts, the bigger the shortfall grows.

Method one gives you a chance of doing better by getting a higher investment return on your pension fund as you are paying interest on the loan. It also gives you a chance of doing worse than the 2% a year or so you must have with method 2.

But remember that the cash sum you can get on a personal pension is restricted to 25% of the sum you have accumulated in your pension fund (up to 37½% at age 75 for a man with a retirement annuity if you have one which can be used). So if you don't pay the interest and let it accumulate, unless your loan back is as little as 25% of your pension fund you are unlikely to have enough money to pay it off from the cash lump sum on retirement. These types of loan backs are better looked at as a means of spending money locked up in property rather than spending your pension fund in advance. So long as you plan to be able to sell the property to pay off the loan back, then the loan back is not jeopardising the value of your pension.

Bank loan back

Some pensions companies do not give loan backs them-selves but have an arrangement with a bank or other lender to make the loan. The loan is also *non status* but the bank normally requires interest to be paid and the interest rate may be rather higher than the other type of loan back. Usually the loan does not have to be repaid until retirement or 75 at latest. Such loan backs are mainly of interest to people who can get tax relief on the interest for a business purpose.

With this type of loan back your pension fund remains in whatever you think is the best type of investment and is never linked to the loan you receive. As you always pay the interest, the loan back works rather like a *pension mortgage* and there is likely to be enough money in your cash lump sum on retirement for you to be able to repay the loan.

The snags

With pension mortgages if you use the cash lump sum to repay your loan you are reducing your potential pension on retirement. With loan backs the extra money you have now is at the expense of money on retirement.

Glossary

Accrual rate The rate at which your pension builds up in a final salary pension scheme. It is often in terms of 60ths of your salary.

Actuarial estimate Mathematical forecast made by insurance specialists called actuaries.

Actuary A specially qualified mathematician employed by insurance and pension companies to work out, among other things, how much money you need to pay now for a pension in the future.

Additional Pension Statement Issued by the Department of Health and Social Security. It lists what your State earnings related (additional) pension is worth at the moment, how much it will be worth when you are 65 for a man, 60 for a woman, and how much your pension will be worth if your earnings average 1.5% a year more than price rises.

Additional State pension See *State earnings related (additional) pension.*

Additional voluntary contributions Contributions paid into a special pension scheme chosen by your employer to top up an existing job pension.

Age allowance An additional tax allowance given to men and women over 65 on below average incomes; it is a larger amount for the over 80's.

Appointed representatives can only sell pensions and other investment services issued by one single company.

Annual report Issued by the pension company every year to show how the investments in your pension fund are performing.

Annuity A life insurance policy which gives the policy-holder an income for life but, usually, without returning any of the original investment.

Association of Futures Brokers & Dealers Authorises commodity and futures dealers under the Financial Services Act.

AVC See *Additional voluntary contributions.*

Average earnings index How much earnings have increased year by year.

Balanced fund See *Managed fund.*

Basic State pension See *State basic (flat rate) pension.*

Benefits What an individual receives from an insurance policy or pension scheme which may be either a lump sum or a pension or both.

Best advice When an *appointed representative* gives best advice, he must offer the best type of pension from the one company he is representing. If his company does not offer a pension suitable for you, he is supposed to say so but cannot recommend another company. When an *independent financial adviser* gives best advice, he must select the best type of pension and the one offering the most suitable benefits from the best of competing pensions companies.

Broker managed fund Similar to a managed fund but where the broad investment strategy and type of investment – sometimes the detailed decisions too – is decided by your own stockbroker, insurance broker or investment adviser who makes an arrangement with a pensions company.

Buy out bond A special type of individual pension fund where you can transfer the value of your pension rights from a job pension. The money accumulates tax free until you retire when it is used to buy a pension.

Capital gains tax The tax you pay on any profit or gain you make when you sell something for more than you buy it for. The first £5,000 in 1988–89 is tax free; the rest is taxed as if it is income. Money in pension funds and paid out of pension funds is exempt from capital gains tax.

Cash deposit fund See *Cash fund.*

Cash fund Consists of contributions paid into special bank or building society accounts or a life insurance fund or unit trust investing in bank or building society accounts.

Cash lump sum See *Lump sum.*

CISR Contracted-in salary related. A final salary job pension which is contracted-in to the State earnings related (Additional) pension.

Company pension Described in this book as a *job pension*, it is a pension scheme run by an employer for his employees.

COMP See *COMPS*.

COMPS Contracted-out money purchase pension scheme. A money purchase job pension which is contracted-out of the State earnings related (additional) pension. See also *Money purchase*.

COSR Contracted-out salary related. A final salary job pension which is contracted-out of the State earnings related (additional) pension. See also *Final salary*.

Contracted-in Employees who contribute to the State earnings related (additional) pension by paying ordinary national insurance. The Department of Health and Social Security calls this *Not contracted-out*.

Contracted-out Employees who do not contribute to the State earnings related (additional) pension because their job pension has contracted-out or who contribute to a contracted-out personal pension.

Contributions Payments. Refers to national insurance contributions and contribution rebate to a pension scheme.

Contributory job pension A pension scheme provided by your employer to which both he and you contribute.

Controlling director A director who owns or controls more than 20% of the company he or she works for.

Corporation tax The tax a company pays on its profits.

Credits When you are unemployed, or sick, you will receive benefit for the State basic pension for national insurance contributions which you have not paid.

Currency cash fund Invests in bank deposits in foreign currencies.

Decreasing term insurance See *Mortgage protection insurance*.

Deposit based pension You pay contributions to a bank or building society which invests your money in your own pension fund where it gains interest. This type of pension is not covered by the Financial Services Act.

Deposit fund Consists of contributions invested in special building society and bank accounts or a life insurance fund or unit trust investing in building society or bank accounts.

DHSS Department of Health and Social Security, the Government department which is responsible for State pensions.

Director's job pension A special pension for directors, sometimes in addition to an ordinary job pension. Also known as an *executive pension* and *top hat pension*.

Disability pension A pension paid to you if you are ill or disabled and unable to work before retirement age.

Dividend An amount paid from the profits of a company to the shareholders.

Earnings limits Weekly, monthly, quarterly and yearly amounts used to determine how much national insurance contributions you pay and to work out the amount of State earnings related (additional) pension. The limits relate to tax years which start on 6 April and are raised each year. For 1988–89 the yearly *lower earnings limit* is £2,132 and the yearly *upper earnings limit* is £15,860.

Earnings related State pension See *State earnings related (additional) pension.*

Earnings rule Your State basic pension is reduced if your earnings come to more than a certain limit between ages 65 and 70 (men) and 60 and 65 (women).

Endowment based with profits pension fund This type of pension guarantees a cash sum on retirement which is used to buy a *pension annuity*. Bonuses are added to this sum each year.

Endowment mortgage A loan to buy a property where you pay interest to a bank or building society and pay premiums for an endowment insurance policy which guarantees to pay you the loan at a given date or when you die.

Equities Stocks and shares.

Equity fund Invests in shares, unit trusts, fixed interest and government stock, overseas shares and unit trusts specialising in overseas shares.

Estate The money and property you leave when you die.

Executive pension A special pension for executives and directors, sometimes in addition to their job pension. Also known as *director's pension* or *top hat pension.*

Family income benefit An insurance policy which pays a regular income to your widow, widower or dependents if you die before the policy expires.

FIMBRA See Financial Intermediaries, Managers and Brokers Regulatory Association.

Final salary pension A pension based on the number of years you belong to it and your pay shortly before you retire. The most you can get is usually around two thirds of your final pay if you have been in the scheme for 40 years (though it is possible to get this after 20 years).

Financial Intermediaries, Managers and Brokers Regulatory Association for independent intermediaries FIMBRA for short, this Association is mainly concerned with the sales of pensions, unit trusts and life insurance and brokers who advise on investment management and investment advice generally.

Financial Services Act Brought into full effect on 1 July 1988, this Act brings in new rules governing most financial and investment advice including pensions and the people who give it.

Fixed interest fund Invests in fixed interest and government stock.

Flat rate State pension See State basic (flat rate) pension.

Free standing additional voluntary contributions
Additional contributions paid into a special pension
scheme you choose which helps top up your existing job
pension. Different from an ordinary additional voluntary
contributions scheme because you can choose the pension
scheme and type of investment instead of your employer
making the choice for you.

FSAVC See *Free standing additional voluntary contributions.*

GMP See *Guaranteed minimum pension.*

Graduated pension An additional State pension which
employees could take during 1961 to 1975. The pension is
based on contributions made during that time.

Group pension scheme A job pension scheme to which
employees of a number of companies belonging to a larger
group can belong.

Group personal pension Where an employer asks a
pension company to offer personal pensions to his staff as
a group.

Guaranteed   minimum   pension The   part   of   a
contracted-out job pension which is paid instead of the
State earnings related (additional) pension.

Guaranteed pension fund See *Non profit pension fund.*

Home responsibilities protection The time you take
off work and not pay national insurance contributions in
order to bring up children or look after someone who is
disabled or very ill without affecting your State pensions.

IMRO See *Investment Managers Regulatory Organisation.*

Incentive payment An extra payment which the DHSS pays into your individual pension if since 6 April 1988 you opt out of the State earnings related (additional) pension and choose a contracted-out pension having not been contracted-out during the previous two years.

Increasing term insurance An insurance policy which pays a lump sum if you die before the policy ends. The lump sum increases at regular periods through the duration of the policy.

Independent financial advisers Advisers who offer a choice of the best pensions products from a number of companies.

Index-linked Gilts fund See *Index-linked stock fund.*

Index-linked stock fund Invests in British Government index-linked stock.

Inflation-linked Any sum of money which rises in line with the Retail Prices Index.

Inheritance tax The tax liable on the money and property you leave when you die. The first £110,000 for 1988–89 is tax free. After that the tax is currently 40%.

Insurance broker Must be registered by the Insurance Brokers' Registration Council.

Insurance Brokers' Registration Council A recognised professional body which authorises insurance brokers. Many insurance brokers will also be members of FIMBRA.

International fund Invests in overseas shares and some UK shares. Some international funds concentrate on particular areas or countries and some on specific sectors of one particular country.

Investment linked fund A fund where your benefits are linked directly to the performance of a fund which is normally divided into units. Also called a *unit linked fund*.

Investment Managers Regulatory Organisation For unit trust and investment managers, the Organisation is concerned with the way in which portfolios are managed, not sales. Also known as *IMRO*.

Job pension Also known as *company* or *occupational* pensions, a pension scheme provided by an employer for his employees.

Know Your Client An expression coined in the Financial Services Act which means all advisers must ask for an adequate amount of financial and personal information from the client.

LAUTRO See *Life Assurance and Unit Trust Regulatory Organisation*.

Life annuity In exchange for a lump sum a life insurance company agrees to pay you an income for the rest of your life or for the rest of your widow's or widower's life if they die after you.

Life Assurance and Unit Trust Regulatory Organisation A self regulatory body which covers sales and marketing by life insurance companies and unit trust management groups. Also known as *LAUTRO*.

Loan back Where you can borrow back the contributions you have made into a pension scheme.

Low cost endowment mortgage Similar to an endowment mortgage but the payments are lower in the first few years. See *Endowment mortgage.*

Lower earnings limit See *Earnings limits.*

Lump sum Sometimes called cash lump sum, the maximum amount of money you can take at once from your pension on retirement. The rest must be paid on a regular basis usually monthly, quarterly, half yearly or yearly.

Managed fund Invests in a mixture of shares and unit trusts, property, fixed interest and cash on deposit.

Mixed fund See *Managed fund.*

Money fund Consists of contributions paid into special bank or building society accounts or unit trusts investing in building societies and banks.

Money purchase pension This type of pension depends on the amount of money paid into it by you and your employer. At retirement the contributions plus interest and capital gains buy an annuity which pays you an income for life.

Mortgage protection insurance Pays off the outstanding loan on a repayment mortgage if you die before the mortgage is repaid. Sometimes called decreasing term insurance.

National insurance contributions Payments made by most working, (earning) people to the State basic (flat rate) pension and in the case of the State earnings related (additional) pension those employees and employers who wish to. You also get sickness and maternity benefit, and employees get unemployment benefit.

Net relevant earnings Earnings on which contributions to a personal pension scheme are worked out.

Non-contributory pension A pension to which only your employer contributes – you, as an employee, pay nothing.

Non profit pension fund Also known as guaranteed pension fund, the pensions linked to these funds offer a fixed rate of return from the date of investment to the date when you have chosen to retire and may also guarantee what your pension will be.

Non status loan A loan which depends on the value of the security eg house, and pension fund and not on your income.

Occupational pension Described in this book as a job pension, it is a pension scheme run by an employer for his employees.

Open market option This allows you to choose which life insurance company you wish to buy your pension annuity from when you retire.

Partnerships When two people agree to run a business together.

PAYE Pay As You Earn. How tax is deducted from

employee's salaries by their employers before they receive their take home pay.

Pension A regular payment received by someone when he or she retires, normally in return for contributions during their working life.

Pension annuity A life insurance policy which buys an income for life, or for the joint lives of a husband or wife, which is bought with the accumulated pension fund on retirement.

Pension fund Where the money which you contribute towards a pension is invested.

Pension mortgage A mortgage which is linked to a pension scheme.

Pensionable earnings Your earnings on which your contributions and working out your final salary is based. Sometimes this is defined as your actual salary less the *lower earnings limit* for national insurance contributions.

Pensions holiday If investments are doing well in a final salary pensions fund, an employer can stop making contributions while the fund is in surplus.

Permanent health insurance Sometimes called sick pay insurance, an insurance policy which pays a regular income, either fixed or increasing, to a chosen retirement date after one to 24 months of disability.

Personal allowance Usually refers to the tax allowance which everyone is entitled to. In 1988–89 tax year, £2,605 for single people, £4,095 for married couple and £2,605 for a working wife.

Personal pension A way of saving towards retirement which is individual to you. It is not tied to a job.

Personal tax allowance See *Personal allowance.*

Polarisation A decision made by the Securities and Investment Board that a person or company selling a pension must either be an Authorised Representative who can sell only pensions from one single company or an Independent Intermediary who offers a choice of the best pensions from all companies.

Premiums Payments paid into an insurance policy or a pension provided by an insurance company.

Preserved pension A job pension which has been left with a previous employer and which you receive at your normal retirement date.

Probate The legal procedure whereby the Government allows the people to whom you leave your money to get it.

Property fund Invests in property or property shares.

Real rate of return The investment return after taking into account inflation. If your pension grows at 10% a year and inflation averages 4% a year, the real return is 6% a year.

Rebate The part of national insurance contributions paid by you and your employer which is passed on by the Department of Health and Social Security into a contracted-out personal pension or the amount by which contributions are reduced if you are contracted-out.

Recognised professional body Certain part time investment advisers can be regulated under the Financial Services Act by their professional body. The main professions covered are chartered accountants, solicitors, insurance brokers and actuaries. Not all members of these professions will necessarily be authorised to give advice. Also known as *RPB*.

Record keeping All advisers must keep records of the advice they give and details of their clients' circumstances.

Reduced rate of national insurance Payable by married women who paid a reduced rate before 1977 and worked without a break of more than two years since then.

Repayment mortgage A loan to buy a property. You pay both interest and repay part of the loan each month.

Residual pension A pension which you get after having taken the lump sum given at retirement age.

Retirement age For State pensions usually 65 for a man, 60 for a woman; the pension can be delayed for up to five years. For personal pensions between ages 50 and 75. For retirement annuities between ages 60 and 75. For job pensions when your employer decides, usually 60 or 65 and no later than 70. You can continue to work after these ages but you must start to draw your pension.

Retirement annuity A life insurance policy which bought an income for life. Was available to the self-employed and people not belonging to a job pension before 1 July 1988. Now available as personal pensions. People who already have a retirement annuity can continue contributing towards it. The rules for lump sums and retirement age are different from a personal pension.

Revalued earnings The amount by which your earnings increase year by year according to an average earnings index for the purpose of working out the State earnings related (additional) pension.

RPB See *Recognised Professional Body.*

Section 32 buy out bond See *Buy out bond.*

Securities and Investment Board Set up by the Government to police most types of investments.

Securities Association A body which authorises stockbrokers.

Self-employed pension The commonly used name for a *Retirement annuity.*

SERPS See *State earnings related (additional) pension.*

SIB See *Securities and Investment Board.*

Sick pay insurance See *Permanent health insurance.*

Simplified job pension scheme A job pension scheme set under special rules which make it easier for an employer to set up.

Sole trader A person who runs a business on his or her own.

SRO Self Regulatory Organisation.

Standing mortgage Where you only pay interest. You do not have to pay back any capital or pay into any endowment or pension scheme. You pay back the loan when you sell the property.

State basic (flat rate) pension If you make enough contributions through your working life, you are entitled to a maximum pension (at 1988–89 rates) of £41.15 a week, £65.90 a week if you are married. A working wife with enough contributions is entitled to her own pension. The pensions are raised every year from 6 April.

State earnings related (additional) pension Also known as SERPS, this pension is only available to employees who contribute through their national insurance contributions. You can choose to leave (to contract-out) or you can stay, in which case you are 'not contracted-out' which is described in this book as *contracted-in*.

State pension See *State basic (flat rate) pension* and *State earnings related (additional) pension*.

Surplus earnings The difference between your average earnings revalued in line with an average earnings index less the lower earnings limit for the tax year before you are 65 years men, 60 years women.

Tax credit An amount of basic rate income tax deemed to be paid when a dividend is paid by a company. A non-tax payer who receives a tax credit can claim it back from the Inland Revenue.

Tax year Runs from 6 April to 5 April of following year.

Term insurance An insurance policy which pays a lump

sum if you die within a certain period fixed when you begin the policy.

3 way fund See *Managed fund.*

Top hat pension A special pension for executives or directors, sometimes in addition to an ordinary job pension. Also called *director's pension* or *executive pension.*

Total surplus earnings See *Surplus earnings.*

Transfer value The amount of money you can move from one pension scheme to another.

Trustee A person responsible for a pension scheme.

Unit-linked pension fund See *Investment linked pension fund.*

Upper earnings limit An amount which the Government fixes every year. See *Earnings limit.*

Wife's earnings allowance The amount of money a wife is allowed to earn before tax is deducted. In the 1988–89 tax year, the allowance is £2,605.

With-profits pension fund Bonuses are added at intervals to the fund. Once added they cannot be taken away.

Working life This term, when referred to by the Department of Health and Social Security, means from age 16 to age 65 for a man, and from age 16 to age 60 for a woman in complete tax years.

Yearly surplus earnings See *Surplus earnings.*

Appendix
How money grows and
inflation reduces its value

The following appendices give details of how money grows
and falls in value at different rates of interest. You can
use them to help calculate how much you need to save
towards a pension and how much that pension will be
worth in today's money.

Appendix 1   How money grows: lump sums

This table shows how much £1,000 will grow to at 2% a year to 7% a year interest over different time periods.

Years	Interest rate 2% £	3% £	4% £	5% £	6% £	7% £
1	1,020	1,030	1,040	1,050	1,060	1,070
2	1,040	1,061	1,082	1,103	1,124	1,145
3	1,061	1,093	1,125	1,158	1,191	1,225
4	1,082	1,126	1,170	1,216	1,262	1,311
5	1,104	1,159	1,217	1,276	1,338	1,403
6	1,126	1,194	1,265	1,340	1,419	1,501
7	1,149	1,230	1,316	1,407	1,504	1,606
8	1,172	1,267	1,369	1,477	1,594	1,718
9	1,195	1,305	1,423	1,551	1,689	1,838
10	1,219	1,344	1,480	1,629	1,791	1,967
11	1,243	1,384	1,539	1,710	1,898	2,105
12	1,268	1,426	1,601	1,796	2,012	2,252
13	1,294	1,469	1,665	1,886	2,133	2,410
14	1,319	1,513	1,732	1,980	2,261	2,579
15	1,346	1,558	1,801	2,079	2,397	2,759
16	1,373	1,605	1,873	2,183	2,540	2,952
17	1,400	1,653	1,948	2,292	2,693	3,159
18	1,428	1,702	2,026	2,407	2,854	3,380
19	1,457	1,754	2,107	2,527	3,026	3,617
20	1,486	1,806	2,191	2,653	3,207	3,870
21	1,516	1,860	2,279	2,781	3,400	4,141
22	1,546	1,916	2,370	2,925	3,604	4,430
23	1,577	1,974	2,465	3,072	3,820	4,741
24	1,608	2,033	2,563	3,225	4,049	5,072
25	1,641	2,094	2,666	3,386	4,292	5,427
30	1,811	2,427	3,243	4,322	5,743	7,612
35	2,000	2,814	3,946	5,516	7,686	10,677
40	2,208	3,262	4,801	7,040	10,286	14,974

This table shows how much £1,000 will grow to at 8% to 13% a year interest over different time periods.

Interest rate 8% £	9% £	10% £	11% £	12% £	13% £	Years
1,080	1,090	1,100	1,110	1,120	1,130	1
1,166	1,188	1,210	1,232	1,254	1,277	2
1,260	1,295	1,331	1,368	1,405	1,443	3
1,360	1,412	1,464	1,518	1,574	1,630	4
1,469	1,539	1,611	1,685	1,762	1,842	5
1,587	1,677	1,772	1,870	1,974	2,082	6
1,714	1,828	1,949	2,076	2,211	2,353	7
1,851	1,993	2,144	2,305	2,476	2,658	8
1,999	2,172	2,358	2,558	2,773	3,004	9
2,159	2,367	2,594	2,839	3,106	3,395	10
2,332	2,580	2,853	3,147	3,479	3,836	11
2,518	2,813	3,138	3,498	3,896	4,335	12
2,720	3,066	3,452	3,883	4,363	4,898	13
2,937	3,342	3,797	4,310	4,887	5,535	14
3,172	3,642	4,177	4,785	5,474	6,254	15
3,426	3,970	4,595	5,311	6,130	7,067	16
3,700	4,328	5,054	5,895	6,866	7,986	17
3,996	4,717	5,560	6,544	7,690	9,024	18
4,316	5,142	6,116	7,263	8,613	10,197	19
4,661	5,604	6,727	8,062	9,646	11,523	20
5,034	6,109	7,400	8,949	10,804	13,021	21
5,437	6,659	8,140	9,934	12,100	14,714	22
5,871	7,258	8,954	11,026	13,552	16,627	23
6,341	7,911	9,850	12,239	15,179	18,788	24
6,848	8,623	10,835	13,585	17,000	21,231	25
10,063	13,268	17,449	22,892	29,960	39,116	30
14,785	20,414	28,102	38,575	52,800	72,069	35
21,725	31,409	45,259	65,001	93,051	132,782	40

Appendix 2   How money grows: yearly investments

This table shows how much £1,000 a year invested in a pension fund grows to at 2% to 7% a year interest over different time periods.

Years	Interest rate 2% £	3% £	4% £	5% £	6% £	7% £
1	1,020	1,030	1,040	1,050	1,060	1,070
2	2,060	2,091	2,122	2,153	2,184	2,215
3	3,122	3,184	3,246	3,310	3,375	3,440
4	4,204	4,309	4,416	4,526	4,637	4,751
5	5,308	5,468	5,633	5,802	5,975	6,153
6	6,434	6,662	6,898	7,142	7,394	7,654
7	7,583	7,892	8,214	8,549	8,897	9,260
8	8,755	9,159	9,583	10,027	10,491	10,978
9	9,950	10,464	11,006	11,578	12,181	12,816
10	11,169	11,808	12,486	13,207	13,972	14,784
11	12,412	13,192	14,026	14,917	15,870	16,888
12	13,680	14,618	15,627	16,713	17,882	19,141
13	14,974	16,086	17,292	18,598	20,015	21,550
14	16,293	17,599	19,024	20,578	22,276	24,129
15	17,639	19,157	20,825	22,657	24,673	26,888
16	19,012	20,762	22,698	24,840	27,213	29,840
17	20,412	22,414	24,645	27,132	29,906	32,999
18	21,841	24,117	26,671	29,539	32,760	36,379
19	23,297	25,870	28,778	32,066	35,786	39,995
20	24,783	27,676	30,969	34,719	38,993	43,861
21	26,299	29,537	33,248	37,500	42,392	48,006
22	27,845	31,453	35,618	40,430	45,996	52,436
23	29,422	33,426	38,083	43,502	49,816	57,177
24	31,030	35,459	40,646	46,727	53,865	62,249
25	32,671	37,553	43,312	50,113	58,156	67,677
30	41,379	49,003	58,328	69,761	83,802	101,073
35	50,994	62,276	76,598	94,836	118,121	147,913
40	61,610	77,663	98,827	126,840	164,048	213,610

This table shows how much £1,000 a year invested in a pension fund grows to at 8% to 13% a year interest over different time periods.

Interest rate 8% £	9% £	10% £	11% £	12% £	13% £	Years
1,080	1,090	1,100	1,110	1,120	1,130	1
2,246	2,278	2,310	2,342	2,374	2,407	2
3,506	3,573	3,641	3,710	3,779	3,850	3
4,867	4,985	5,105	5,228	5,353	5,480	4
6,336	6,523	6,716	6,913	7,115	7,323	5
7,923	8,200	8,487	8,783	9,089	9,405	6
9,637	10,028	10,436	10,859	11,300	11,757	7
11,488	12,021	12,579	13,164	13,776	14,416	8
13,487	14,193	14,937	15,722	16,549	17,420	9
15,645	16,560	17,531	18,561	19,665	20,814	10
17,977	19,141	20,384	21,708	23,133	24,650	11
20,495	21,953	23,523	25,212	27,029	28,985	12
23,215	25,019	26,975	29,095	31,393	33,883	13
26,152	28,361	30,772	33,405	36,280	39,417	14
29,324	32,003	34,950	38,190	41,753	45,672	15
32,750	35,974	39,545	43,501	47,884	52,739	16
36,450	40,301	44,599	49,396	54,750	60,725	17
40,446	45,018	50,159	55,939	62,440	69,749	18
44,762	50,160	56,275	63,203	71,052	79,947	19
49,423	55,765	63,002	71,265	80,699	91,470	20
54,457	61,873	70,403	80,214	91,503	104,491	21
59,893	68,532	78,543	90,148	103,603	119,205	22
65,765	75,790	87,497	101,174	117,155	135,831	23
72,106	83,701	97,347	113,413	132,334	154,620	24
78,954	92,324	108,182	126,999	149,334	175,850	25
122,346	148,575	180,943	220,913	270,293	331,315	30
186,102	235,125	298,127	379,164	483,463	617,749	35
279,781	368,292	486,852	645,827	859,142	1,145,486	40

Source: The Savers and Investors Guide 1988–89

Appendix 3   How inflation reduces the value of your money

This table shows how much £1,000 in the future will be worth in today's money at 2% to 7% a year inflation over different time periods.

Years	Inflation rate					
	2% £	3% £	4% £	5% £	6% £	7% £
1	980	971	962	952	943	935
2	961	943	925	907	890	873
3	942	915	889	864	840	816
4	924	888	855	823	792	763
5	906	863	822	784	747	713
6	888	837	790	746	705	666
7	871	813	760	711	665	623
8	853	789	731	677	627	582
9	837	766	703	645	592	544
10	820	744	676	614	558	508
11	804	722	650	585	527	475
12	788	701	625	557	497	444
13	773	681	601	530	469	415
14	758	661	577	505	442	388
15	743	642	555	481	417	362
16	728	623	534	458	394	339
17	714	605	513	436	371	317
18	700	587	494	416	350	296
19	686	570	475	396	331	277
20	673	554	456	377	312	258
21	660	538	439	356	294	242
22	647	522	422	342	278	226
23	634	507	406	326	262	211
24	622	492	390	310	247	197
25	610	478	375	295	233	184
30	552	412	308	231	174	131
35	500	355	253	181	130	94
40	453	307	208	142	97	67

s table shows how much £1,000 in the future will be worth
oday's money at 8% to 13% a year inflation over different
e periods.

ation rate						Years
	9% £	10% £	11% £	12% £	13% £	
5	917	909	901	893	885	1
7	842	826	812	797	783	2
4	772	751	731	712	693	3
5	708	683	659	636	613	4
4	650	621	593	567	543	5
0	596	564	535	507	480	6
3	547	513	482	452	425	7
0	502	467	434	404	376	8
0	460	424	391	361	333	9
3	422	386	352	322	295	10
9	388	350	314	287	261	11
7	356	319	286	257	231	12
3	326	290	258	229	204	13
0	299	263	232	205	181	14
5	275	239	209	183	160	15
2	252	218	188	163	141	16
0	231	198	170	146	125	17
0	212	180	153	130	111	18
2	194	164	138	116	98	19
5	178	149	124	104	87	20
9	164	135	112	93	77	21
4	150	123	101	83	68	22
0	138	112	91	74	60	23
3	126	102	82	66	53	24
5	116	92	74	59	47	25
9	75	57	44	33	26	30
3	49	36	26	19	14	35
5	32	22	15	11	8	40

Source: The Savers and Investors Guide 1988–89

Appendix 4
The Financial Services Act

On 1 July 1988 the Financial Services Act which governs investment advice and the people who give it came fully into effect. Summarised here are the different organisations which control the advisers and the companies which sell investments.

The Securities and Investment Board has been set up to police most types of investments. Virtually everyone who wants to sell investments or give investment advice must either be authorised by The Securities and Investment Board (SIB) or be a member of a Self Regulatory Organisation (SRO) or be a qualified member of a Recognised Professional Body (RPB) or be an appointed representative of a firm which is authorised by or is a member of one of the above organisations.

The five self-regulatory organisations are:

● FIMBRA (Financial Intermediaries, Managers & Brokers Regulatory Association for independent intermediaries) who are mainly concerned with the sales of pensions, unit trusts and life insurance and brokers who advise on investment management and investment advice generally.

● IMRO (Investment Management Regulatory Organisation for unit trust and investment managers) who are
concerned with the way in which portfolios are managed,
not sales.

● LAUTRO (Life Assurance & Unit Trust Regulatory
Organisation) which covers sales and marketing by life
insurance companies and unit trust management groups.

● The Securities Association which authorises stockbrokers.

● The Association of Futures Brokers & Dealers which
authorises commodity and futures dealers.

Companies which give investment advice or offer
investment products don't have to belong to these self-
regulatory organisations. They can instead be authorised
directly by the Securities and Investment Board. This
means that one building society acting as an intermediary
may belong to FIMBRA whilst another may be authorised
directly by the Securities and Investment Board.

Chartered and certified accountants, solicitors,
actuaries and insurance brokers are the main individuals
and firms who belong to Recognised Professional Bodies.
If more than 25% of their income comes from investment
business they must also belong to FIMBRA or be
authorised by the Securities and Investment Board.

Companies from countries in the European Community
which the Government agrees has an equivalent regulatory system can also offer pensions but this is not likely to
apply for some time.

All these firms and individuals are subject to tough new
rules over the way in which they sell and market
investments including pensions. There is one exception as
far as pensions are concerned: banks and building

societies which offer personal pensions which they hold as deposits on which they give you interest do not come under the Financial Services Act although you can still complain about them to the Building Societies Ombudsman or Banking Ombudsman. However pensions sold by banks and building societies which are acting as agents for other organisations, for example, life insurance companies, do come under the Act.

Index

A

'About Your Additional Pension' (DHSS letter) 61–3

accountants 17, 123, 194, **207**
    trading status advice 127

accounting year (self-employed) 121

accrual/accrual rate 79–80, **181**

actuarial estimate 144, **181**

actuaries 144, 150, **181**, 194, 207

Additional Pension *see* State pension, earnings-related

Additional Pension Statement 61, **181**

additional voluntary contributions (AVC) 20–21, 27, **94–100**, **182**
    advice 151
    choice of schemes 98, 154–5
    contribution limits 96
    free-standing (FSAVC) 20–21, **98–9**, **187–8**
        lump sum 34
        Minimum contributions 99
        pension choice 154–5
        simplified job pension 145
    lump sum 34, 97
    non-contributory pension 83
    and retirement date 39
    simplified job pension 145

Additional Voluntary Contribution 151

advice/advisers **13–17**, **149–51**, 194, **206–8**
    'best advice' **14–16**, **183**
    commission system **150–51**
    directors 123, 137–8
    employer-sponsored 148
    'know your client' 16, 190
    opting-out of occupational pension 100
    polarisation 14, **193–4**
    record-keeping 16, **194**
    setting up occupational pension 140
    trading status advice 127

age,
   and annuity pension amount 30, 32 *table*
   and contribution limits 24, 26 *table*
   and final salary schemes 144–5
   and investment choice 115
   and job-changing 95
   and life assurance 166, 169 *Table*
   and lump sum 118–19
   and non-profit schemes 103
   and occupational pension 80, 92
   and pension awareness 11–12, 140
   and pension mortgage 173
   and preserved pension 157–9
   and retirement annuity premiums 117–18
   and retirement income tax 36, 37–8
   and retirement tax allowance 136–7
   of retirement *see* retirement
   and State basic pension 42
   and State earnings-related pension 45–7
age allowance **136–7**, **182**
annual report (pension company) **182**
annuities 30, **182**
   life 37–8, 190
   pension *see* pension annuity
   retirement *see* retirement annuities
appointed agents/representatives **14–15**, **182**, 183, 193–4, **206**
Association of Futures Brokers and Dealers **182**, **207**
authorised agents/representatives *see* appointed agents
AVC *see* additional voluntary contributions
average earnings index 45, **182**, 197

B
balanced fund *see* mixed fund
banks,
   as agents 103
   investment-linked schemes 108
   loan-back 179
   penalty charges 103
   pension advice **14–15**, 17
   pension forecasts 64
   pension funds **102–3**
   as pension providers 13
   regulation 207–8
   repayment mortgages 174
   trading status advice 127
basic pension *see* State pension, basic
benefits **182**
   limits on 24, 27, 33, 93
benefits-in-kind/fringe benefits, 87, 125
'best advice' concept **14–16**, **183**
bonus (earnings) 80–81, 96, 125
bonus, (insurance schemes) **104–6**, 186, 198
   final/terminal 153
broker-managed funds **114–15**, **183**

building societies 103, 174
   advice **14–15**, 17
   as agents 103
   AVC scemes 98
   investment-linked schemes 108
   occupational pension 139–48
   pension forecasts 64
   pension funds **102–3**
   as pension providers 13
   regulation 207–8
buy-out bond 101, **162**, **183**

C

capital gains tax **183**
cash deposit fund/cash fund/money fund 102–3, **108**, **183**
'cash' lump sum/payment *see* lump sum
charity, occupational pension 139–48
child, *see* dependant
CISP *see* contracted-in: salary-related
Citizens Advice Bureaux 47, 57, 61
commission payments (directors) 125
company, advantages/disadvantages **127–31**
company directors *see* directors
company pension *see* occupational pension
COMP/COMPS *see* contracted-out: money purchase schemes
compound bonus rate 105
Consumer Credit Act 175
Consumer Association Ltd 151
contracted in (not-contracted-out), occupational pension **81–3**
contracted in (not-contracted-out) 53, **141–3**, **184**, 197
contracted in (not-contracted-out),
   money purchase schemes 21
   salary-related (CISR) **183–4**
contracted-in/-out, combined 142
contracted-out 53, **142–3**, **184**, 197
   additional voluntary contributions (AVC) 99–100
   former contributors 63
   as incentive 142
   money purchase schemes (COMP/COMPS) 21, 138, **184**
   not-contracted-out *see* contracted-in
   occupational pension **81–3**
   salary-related (COSR) 184
   simplified job pension 145, 146
   transfer 159–60
   see also State pension, earnings-related: opting-out
contributions,
   (*defined*) **184**
   limits on **24–7**, 26–7
   voluntary,
      to occupational pension 20–21
      to state basic pension 19
      see also additional voluntary contributions
contributory pension scheme, *defined* 20, **184**
controlling director 161–2, **184**

corporation tax **185**
COSR (contracted-out salary-related) **184**
credits (NI) **185**
credit (tax) **197**
currency cash fund **109, 185**

D

death,
    before insurance term 168–71
    before retirement **88–9**, 153
    continuation of pension 86–7
    see also insurance
decreasing term insurance 167 (*see also* mortgage protection insurance)
Department of Health and Social Security *see* DHSS
dependants,
    insurance 165–71
    occupational pension 86–7, 88–9, 165
    probate 168–70
    State pension, basic 41–2
    see also wife *etc*
deposit-based pensions 64, **185**
    loan-back 178–9
    pension forecasts 64
    pension fund **102–3**, 153
deposit fund 102–3, **185**
DHSS (Department of Health and Social Security) 185
    Additional Pension Statement 61, 181
    earnings-related pensions 47, 61–3
    enquiry offices 47, 57, 61
    leaflets **57–8** (*see also individual titles*)
    NI contributions information 53, 62
directors,
    controlling 161–2, **184**
    National Insurance contributions 53
    occupational pension 20, 21, 93, 139
    transfer 156, 161–2
    see also employers
director's/executive pension 137, 150, 151, **185, 186–7**
Director's Retirement Plan/Director Finance Account 137
disability pension **89–90**, **185**
dividend, (*defined*) **185**, 197
divorced couples, State basic pension 43

E

earnings,
    average, index of 45, **182**, 197
    net relevant **191**
    pensionable **80–81**, 87, 95, 165, **193**
    revalued 45, **195**
    surplus 45, **197**
earnings limits **185** (see also low *and* upper earnings limit)
earnings-related pension, occupational *see* final salary schemes
earnings-related pension, State *see* State pension, earnings-related
earnings rule **186**

State pensions **54–5**
employees,
    overseas 43–4, 207
    without pension 21–2, **57–76**
    see also occupational pension
employers,
    group personal pension 147–8
    occupational pension **139–48**
    pension contributions 30, 26–7, 123–4
    small company options 20
    State earnings-related pension 47
    see also directors
employment termination, compensation 125
endowment-based with-profits schemes **105–6**, **186**
endowment mortgage 174
equities, (*defined*) **186**
equity fund **112–13**, **186**
estate, (*defined*) 170, **186**
executive pension 137, **196–7** (*see also* director's pension)
Executive Pensions 1987–88 (Lewis) 137, 151
Executive Pensions 1988–89 151
Executive Retirement Plan 137

F
Fact Sheet About Your Additional Pension Statement, A (DHSS: *NP38*)
61–3
family income benefit (insurance) 89, 167, **187**
FIMBRA *see* Financial Intermediaries, Managers *etc* Association
final bonus 153
final salary scheme 20, 33, **78–81**, **187**
    advantages/disadvantages **143–5**
    CISR 183–4
    COSR 184
    director's pension 125
    lump sum 33–4, 35 *table*
    and opting-out of occupational pension 93
    preserved pension 157–9
    simplified job pension **146–7**
    small businesses 21
    transfer from 161
    transfer to **160–61**
final/terminal bonus, 104, 106
financial information, personal 16, 190
Financial Intermediaries, Managers and Brokers Regulatory
Association (FIMBRA) 17, 150, **187**, **206**, 207
Financial Services Act 182, **187**, **206–8**
    deposit-based pension 185
    effective dates 13, 19, 187
    investment advice 13
    opted-out of State scheme 66–8
    pension forecasts 63–4
    pensions advisers 100, 190, 194
    pensions providers 13, 14
Financial Times Business Information Ltd 137, 151–2

fixed-interest funds **109–10**, **111**, **187**
flat rate pension **see** State pension, basic; guaranteed pension
foreign countries, pension arrangements 43–4, 207
foreign currency investment 109, 111
foreign shares *see* international funds
free-standing AVC *see* additional voluntary contributions
fringe benefits, occupational pension 87, 125
FSAVC *see* additional voluntary contributions: free-standing

G

Gilts 108, 109
GMP (guaranteed minimum pension) 158
graduated pension (State) 41, **188**
gross profile mortgage repayment 174
group pension scheme 139, **188**
group personal pension 21, **147–8**, **188**
guaranteed minimum pension (GMP) 158
guaranteed pension **86**, 103, 153, **192**

H

home responsibilities protection 42, **49–52**, **188**

I

illness *see* sick pay; disability; *and* retirement: health reasons
IMRO *see* Investment Managers Regulatory Organisation
incentive (NI) 66, 70, **71**, 142, **188**
    additional voluntary contributions (AVC) 99
    and occupational pension 83
income tax *see* tax
increasing family income benefit 167
increasing term insurance 166–7, **189**
independent advisers/intermediaries **13–15**, 183, **189**, 194
index-linked pension 30, 32 *table*, **85–8**
index-linked stock/Gilts fund **108–9**, **189**
index-linking,
    earnings limits 71
    insurance policies 167
    State pensions, 42, 56
    see also inflation
Individual Pension Plan 137
inflation **204–5 *table***
    personal pension 65, 67
    rate of return 194
    rising pensions **85–6**
    State pension, earnings-related (additional) 63, 65–6
    transfer value 157–8
    see also index-linking
inflation-linking 12, **189**
inheritance tax 170, 171, **189**
insurance brokers 17, **150**, **189**, 194, **207**
    managed funds 114–15, 183
Insurance Brokers Registration Council 150, **189**
insurance companies,
    AVC schemes 98

buy-out-bonds 162
deposit-based funds 102–3
pension, annuity, occupational pension 20
as pension providers 13
required for pension annuity 31
retirement annuities **117**
with-profits schemes 104–6
insurance/life assurance **165–71**
annuity *see* annuities
employer-sponsored 140, **148**, 156
illness/disability **89–90**
limitations on 165–6, 168
linked to personal pension 87
mortgage-linked 172–5 (*see also* mortgage)
as occupational pension fringe benefit **87**, 89
penalty charges 98, 99
premiums, duration 165, 166, 167, 169 *table*, 173
premiums, increasing 166–7
premiums, refunded 170–71
tax relief 24
types of policy 166–7
interest-based with-profit schemes **104–5**, 105–6
international fund **113–4**, **189**
investment advisers, managed funds 114–15, 183
investment-linking **106–15**, **189–90**
assessment of 152–4, 155
charges 106–7, 153–4
loan-back 176, 178–9
unit-linked fund 102–3
Investment Managers Regulatory Organisation (IMRO) **190**, **206–7**
investments **101–15**
choice of 115
growth charts **200–205** *table*
risk **107–8**
taxable/tax-free 13, **27–9**
types of **107–8**

J
job-changing **156–64**
additional voluntary contributions (AVC) 98
group personal pension 147
personal pensions 21
see also transfer
job pension *see* occupational pensions
joint life pension 136

K
'know your client' concept 16, **190**

L
LAUTRO *see* Life Assurance *etc* Organisation
Lewis, David 137, 151
life annuity, 37–8, **190**
Life Assurance and Unit Trust Regulatory Organisation (LAUTRO)

150–51, **190**, **207**
life insurance, *see* insurance companies
loan-back 172, **175–80**, **190**
    interest 177–9
    limitations 178
    security 175–6
low cost endowment mortgage **190**
lower earnings limit 44, 66, 71, 185, 193, 197
    additional voluntary contributions (AVC) 96
    and occupational pension 81
lump sum **31–4**, **37–8**, **191**
    additional voluntary contributions (AVC) 97
    advantages 37–8
    buy-out-bonds 162
    contribution timing 122
    growth charts **200–201** *table*
    life assurance 105, 165–71
    loan-back 179
    mortgage-linked 173, 174
    occupational pension **33–4**, **35** *table*, 38
    open market option 163
    opted-out of State scheme 67, **68–70**
    personal pension **33**
    retirement annuity 117, **118–19**
    simplified job pension 146
    tax 37–8
    trivial pension 164

M
managed funds *see* mixed funds
married allowance 132
maturing, of stock, (*defined*) 109
minimum contribution personal pension **66–70**, 82, 100
mixed/managed/3-way/balanced funds **111–12**, 114–15, **191**
money fund 102–3, **191** (*see also* cash deposit funds)
money purchase schemes 20, **191**
    contracted-out (COMP/COMPS) 184
    early retirement 84–5
    free-standing AVC 20
    investments **101–2**
    occupational pension 21, **81**, 82, **143–5**
        maxima 33–4, **35** *table*
    simplified job pension 145–6
    transfer 159, **161**
mortgage **174–5**
    as loan-back security 175–7
    pension *see* pension mortgage
mortgage protection/decreasing term insurance 167, **191**

N
National Insurance (NI) contributions **52–3**, **54** *table*, **55** *table*, **191**
    company 129–32, 133 *table*
    credit 185
    duration **135**

employee 130
employers 130, 132
    contracted-out employees 142–3
group personal pension 147
husband-and-wife **131–2**, **133** *table*
limits on 131
lump sum 33
occupational pension, savings 141–2, 145, 146
partners 129
for personal pension 59, 66–8, **70–71**
qualifying years **49–52**
reduced rate 42–3, **52**, 53, **195**
retirement income 34
self-employed **129**, **131–2**, **133** *table*
sole traders 129
and State basic pension 18–19, **42**
statement 62
voluntary 43, **53**
National Insurance Voluntary Contributions (DHSS: *NI142*) 53, 58
net relevant earnings **191**
NI *see* National Insurance
non-contributory pension 20, **83–4**, 96–7, **141–2**, **192**
non-employed persons, voluntary contributions 19
non-profit/ guaranteed pension **86**, **103**, 153, **192**
non-status loan 176, 179, **192**
non-contracted-out *see* contracted-in

O
occupational pension **19–21**, **77–93**, 192
    additional contributions *see* additional voluntary contributions
    assessment of 76
    benefit limits 79, 80, **93**, 126 *table*
        director's pension 124-5
        simplified job penson 146
    benefit statement 78
    buying-out 183
    changes to 94–5, **148**
    contracted-in/-out **81–3**
    contribution amounts 20
    contribution limits 78, 127, 128, 145
    contributions refunded **164**
    contributory, (*defined*) 184
    COSR 184
    costs 140–41
    date of joining 124–5
    director's **123–38**, 137–8
    employers **139–48**
    as incentive 140, 143, 147–8
    information booklet 77–8
    insurance 165, 166, 168
    legal requirements 77–8
    lump sum 38
    mortgage/loan-back 172
    non-contributory 20, **83–4**, 96–7, **141–2**, **192**

non-shareholder organisation 139–48
opting-out, for and against 90–93
as pay-rise substitute 141–2
pension fund annual report 78
pension fund limits 78
setting-up of **140–48**, 150
simplified scheme 196
supplemented, *see* additional voluntary contributions
trading status 127
transfer **156–64** (*see also* transfer)
trustees 140, 144, 160–61, 198
types of **78–84**
voluntary contributions *see* additional voluntary contributions
Occupational Pensions Board, 1981 report 12
older people *see* age
open market option **31**, **163**, **192**
opting out,
    of occupational pension scheme 19–20 (*see also* transfer)
    of State earnings-related scheme, 19, **22**, 33, 39 (*see also* contracted-out)
overtime payments 80–81, 96

P
partners/partnerships 53, **116–22**, 139, **192**
    status options 127–31
PAYE (Pay As You Earn) 36, **192**
pension 23, **149–55**, **192**
    buy-out-bonds 161, **162**, **183**
    comparative surveys 151–2
    do-nothing option 76
    duration of benefits **86–7**
    forecasts 61–4
    frequency of payment 30
    heritable 30, 86–7
    increasing 30, 31, 32 *table*
    individual *see* personal pension
    loan-back 172, **175–80**, **190**
    multiple 22, 51
    objectives 11–17
    revalued 158, 160
    trivial 164
    types of **18–22**
Pensionable earnings **80–81**, 87, 165, **193**
    State basic pension excluded 95
pension account *see* pension fund
pension annuity 20, **192–3**
    benefit amount **30–31**
    bequeathed 30
    fixed term 30
    and interest rates **31**
    investments **102**
    open market option 163, 192
    opted-out of State scheme 67–8
    retirement annuity 119

pension companies **149–55**
    annual report 132
    charges 153–4, 161, 163, 176
    loan-back 175–9
    occupational pension 140
    takeovers 155
pension fund **193**
    annual report 182
    and annuity 30–31
    assessment of 152–4
    growth of **101–15**, 200–205 *table*
    individual 20, 81
    loan-back 175–80
    surpluses 144
pension mortgage 167, **172–5, 180, 193**
pension providers **13**, 14, 25, **206–8** (*see also* pension companies)
pensions advisers *see* advice
pensions brokers 123
pensions consultant 150
pension holiday 144, **193**
'pension trap' concept 12
'perks' *see* benefits-in-kind
permanent health/sick pay insurance **89–90**, 193
personal allowance **193**
personal pension **21–2, 193**
    contributions refunded 164
    contributions timing 120–22
    DHSS contributions summary 72–3
    directors **123–38**
    forecasts 63–4
    free-standing AVC 187–8
    group 21, **147–8, 188**
    life assurance 165–71
    minimum contribution, **66–70**, 82, 100
    mortgage/loan-back 172–80
    and retirement annuities **117–22**
    and State earnings-related scheme contributions 19
    trading status 127
    transfer from **162–3**
    transfer from **161–2**
Personal Pensions 1988–89 151
personal tax allowance **193**
polarisation 14, **193–4**
policy, pension *see* retirement annuities
Post Offices 47, 57, 61
premiums 117, **194**
preserved pension 95, 157–9, 161, **194**
probate 168–70, 171, **194**
property fund **110–11, 194**
protected rights pension 70
public sector pension schemes 12, 77, **79**
pure endowment scheme 105

R

rate of return,
    real **194**
    standardised projections 64
    rebate (NI) 66, 70, **71**, 142, **194**
    simplified job pension 145
    tax relief 72
Recognised Professional Body (RPB) **194**, 206, **207**
record keeping, advisers 16, **194**
reduced rate *see* National Insurance
repayment mortgage 173, **195**
residual pension 119, **195**
Retail Price Index 189
retirement,
    age at **38–40**, **195**
        occupational pension **84–5**
        opted-out of State schemes 66–7
        retirement annuities 120, 163
        simplified job pension 145–6
        State pensions **54–5**
    compensation for employment termination 125
    date of, pension mortgage 173
    deferred **54–5**, 66–7
    early,
        compulsory 84
        occupational pension 84–5
        opted-out of State schemes 66–7
    for health reasons 39, 84, 185
    occupational pension, maxima 94
retirement annuities 21, 24, **117–22**, 152, **195**
    conrtribution limits 117–18
    contributions timing 118, 120–22
    mortgage/loan-back 172–80
    versus personal pension 118–9
    trading status 127–8
    transfer from **163**
revalued earnings 45, **195**
revalued pension 158, 160
reversionary bonus rate 105
rising pension
    early retirement 40
    occupational pension **85–6**
    opted-out of State scheme 67
rising pensions, retirement annuities 118, **119**
RPB *see* Recognised Professional Body

S

salary,
    final *see* final salary
    high, transfer limitations 161–2
    low, directors 124, 131, 135
    see also earnings
Section 32 buy-out bond 161, **162**, 183
Securities Association **196**

Securities and Investment Board (SIB) 153, 193, **196, 206**, 207
Securities Organisation **207**
self-employed, 21, **116–22**, 151–2
    husband-and-wife **131–8**
    National Insurance contributions 53, **55** *table*
    retirement annuities *see* retirement annuities
    status options 127–31
    see also employers
Self-Employed Pension 1987–88 (Walford) 151–2
Self-employed pension *see* retirement annuity
Self-Regulatory Organisation (SRO) **196, 206–7**
separated couples, State basic pension 43
SEPRS (State Earnings Related Pension Scheme) *see* State pension, earnings-related
severance pay *see* employment: termination
sex,
    and annuity pension amount 30
    and income tax 36–7
    and life assurance 166, 169 *table*
    and lump sum 118–9
    and open market option 163
    opted-out of State scheme 67–8
    and pension amount 32 *table*
    and reduced rate contributions 42–3
    and retirement ananuities 118, **119**
    and retirement income tax 37–8
    and State earnings-related pension 45–7
share ownership, directors 125
SIB *see* Securities and Investment Board
sick pay **89–90**
    NI credits 185
    as occupational pension fringe benefit 87, 89
sick pay insurance **89–90**, **193**
simple bonus rate 105
simplified job pension **145–7, 196**
simplified money purchase schemes 21
small businesses 21, **123–38**
    occupational pension **139–48**
    status options **127–31**
sole traders 53, **116–22**, 139, **196**
    status options 127–31
solicitors 17, 194, **207**
SRO *see* Self-Regulatory Organisation
staff pension *see* occupational pension
standing mortgage 173, **175**, 175, **196**
State pension **41–58**
    additional *see* earnings-realted *below*
    deferred **54–5**
    graduated 41, **188**
    information leaflets **57–8**
    maxima 55–6
State pension, basic (flat rate) **18–19, 41–4, 196–7**
    dependants 41–2
    earnings rule 186

home responsibilities protection 42, **49–52**, **188**
minimum 42
and occupational pension 81
reduced 186
State pension, earnings-related (additional) (SERPS) **18–19**, **44–9**, 50–51 *table*, **197**
    Additional Pension Statement 181
    benefit reduction 60
    buying-back-in 159–60
    effective dates 44–7
    eligible workers 44
    example 47–9, **73–5**
    guaranteed minimum pension 158
    opting out **59–76**
    opting-out,
        advantages/disadvantages **64–6**
        AVC 99–100
        back-dated 70
        directors 130
        method **70–73**, **75**
    and personal pensions 22
    self-employed **116**
State Statutory Sick Pay Scheme **89**
stockbrokers, managed funds 114–15, 183
student, State basic pension 43
sum insured (pension schemes) 105
surplus earnings 45, **197**

T
tax,
    allowances for pension contributions (*defined*) 24
    back-dated 121–2
    buy-out-bonds 162
    capital gains 183
    carried forward 24–5, 121–2
    company 130, 140–41
    contributions refund 164
    corporation 185
    credit on dividend 197
    directors 130, 135
    exemption 13, **27–9**
    guaranteed pension 87
    home-purchase 173
    husband-and-wife 132–4
    inheritance 189
    and loan-back 176
    loan interest 177, 179
    lump sum 37–8
    not relevant earnings (*defined*) 24
    'paid' (*defined*) 27
    PAYE 192
    pension funds 183
    pension mortgage 173–4
    personal allowance 193

relief **23–9**
    additional voluntary contributions (AVC) 98, 99
    as if last year 25–6
    employers 140–41
    life assurance **165–71**, 165–7, **168–71**
    opted-out of State scheme 70, **72–3**
retirement annuities 118, 119, **120**, **121–2**
retirement income **34–8**
    allowances, disability 36
    allowances, personal 34–6
    allowances, wife's 36–7
    deducted at source 36
    State pensions 36
self-employed **120–22**, 130, **132–4**, 135
small businesses 127–31
year, financial 185, **197**
terminal bonus 153
term insurance 166–7, 169 *table*, **197**
    mortgage-linked 173, 175
three-way fund *see* mixed fund
top hat pension *see* executive pension
total surplus earnings 45, **197**
transfer 12, 77, 140
    and final salary schemes 144
    impracticable 156
    limitations on 161–2
    lump sum 97
    non-contributory pension 83–4
    and retirement date 39
    see also job-changing
transfer value **198**
    guaranteed 160–61
    years-for-years 160
trivial amount 164
trust, discretionary, company insurance benefits 87
trustees 198
    occupational pension 140, 144
        transfer value 160–61
    personal pension life policy 170
trust form 170

U
employed, credits 185
unitised with-profits schemes 104–6
unit-linked fund 102–3 (*see also* investment-linking)
unit trusts 13, **102–3**, 107–8
upper earnings limit 44, 63, 71, 185, **198**

V
varying payments mortgage repayment 174

W
wages *see* earnings; salary
Walford, Janet 152

Which? (magazine) 151
widow/widower 30, 165–71
    joint life pension 136
    life annuity 190
    occupational pension 86–7, 8809, 165
    opted-out of State scheme 67
    probate 168–70
    State basic pension 43
wife,
    earnings allowance 36–7, 132, **198**
    earnings-based pension **36–7**
    NI, reduced rate **195**
    personal tax allowance 37
    separate taxation **134**, 136
    state basic pension 41–2, 43, 197
    see also tax; National Insurance; widow
will/bequest 30, 86–7, 170
with-profits schemes 30, 31, **104–6**, **186**, **198**
    assessment of 152–3
    charges 153
    and pension amount 32 *table*
woman,
    State basic pension, reduced 51
    State pension, earnings-related 48
    see also sex; wife
working life, (*defined*) 42, **198**
work pension *see* occupational pension

Y
yearly surplus earnings 45, **197**
years-for-years transfer basic 160, 161
young workers *see* age
Your Future Pension (DHSS: *NP38*) 47, 58, 61, 116